Floating Stones

Great Pyramid Built With Water Power

Samuel R. Sampson
&
Michael N. Read

Oakfield Publishers, Salem, Oregon

Oakfield Publishers
3373 Willamette Dr. N
Salem, Oregon 97303

www.oakfieldpublishers.com

www.FloatingStonesBook.com

ISBN 978-0-615-40872-9

Credits and Permissions

The Authors obtained some of the images used in this book from various sources on the Internet. They diligently wrote to all websites enquiring if the images were the property of the website and asking for permission to use and cite the sources for each image. All of the respondents with ownership rights gave their permission, for which we thank them here. However, many of our inquiries were never responded to, so we have cited all the sources, links and dates of acquisition under each image/quote and claim fair use under the applicable copyright laws.

Cover image: "Great Pyramid under Construction" by Bill Munns using Bryce 6 - wmunns@verizon.net

Here's hoping...

our book will be the start of a new dialogue about the Great Pyramid and Ancient Egypt that encourages your participation.

You're invited...

to experience the story in its entirety by "connecting the dots" of supporting evidence and to comment on any aspect of our book at:

www.floatingstonesbook.com

&

www.oakfieldpublishers.com

Thank you...

for purchasing and reading our book!

CONTENTS

INTRODUCTION   1

SAM'S PREFACE   5

MIKE'S PREFACE   7

BACKGROUND – ANCIENT EGYPT   9

Chapter 1 – River Nile and its Geology   *11*
  The River Nile   11
  Lake Tana in Ethiopia   13
  Nile Flow Rate   14
  Nubian Aquifer   15
  Artesian Wells   15
  Nile Source Elevations   17
  Sahara Desertification   17

Chapter 2 – Resources and Skills   *19*
  Agriculture   19
  Boats and Transportation   20
  Boat Construction   22
  Boats and Boat Pits   23
  Sadd-Al-Kafara Dam   25
  Wells and Rock Drilling   26
  Water under the Giza Plateau   27
  The Quarries   28
  Gypsum   30

PHASE 1 CONSTRUCTION   31

Lower Pyramid Elements   *32*

Chapter 3 – Site Selection, Survey and Preparation   *33*
  Site Selection   33
  Artesian Well   36
  Site Survey   37
  Site Leveling   38
  Other Site Work   39

Chapter 4 – Lower Pyramid Elements   *40*
  Well and Grotto   42
  Descending Corridor   43
  The Subterranean Chamber   44

Chapter 5 – Causeway Delivery System   *47*
  Valley Temple   48
  Causeway and Locks   49
  Mortuary Temple   52
  Enclosure Wall   53

      Other Causeway Systems   54

Chapter 6 – First Seven Courses   *59*
    Enclosure Wall Construction   59
    Enclosure Pond   60
    Font Pond   60
    First Seven Courses   61

Chapter 7 – Phase 1 Water Flow   *63*
    Volume of Water Required   63
    Artesian Well Flow Rates   64
    Water Course   64

PHASE 2 CONSTRUCTION   **67**

Upper Pyramid Elements   *68*

Chapter 8 – Water Stairs   *69*
    Herodotus   69
    Design   71
    Font Pond   75
    Dynamics and Performance   76

Chapter 9 – Pyramid Design   *79*
    Design Characteristics   79
    Entrance Door   80
    Ascending Corridor   81
    Queen's Chamber Horizontal Corridor   83
    Queen's Chamber   84
    Grand Gallery   89
    King's Chamber Horizontal Corridor   92
    King's Chamber   92

Chapter 10 – Pyramidian and Final Finishing   *97*
    Pyramidian   97
    Pyramidian Size   97
    Final Working Platform   99
    Casing Stones   100
    Prefabricated Construction   101
    Cornerstones   102

Chapter 11 – Phase 2 Water Flow   *105*
    Upward Flow   105
    Downward Flow   109
    Stopping the Flow   110
    Remnants of Flow   112

Chapter 12 – Levels of Evidence   *115*
    Circumstantial   116
    Historical   117
    Physical   118
    Implications   120

APPENDICES   **125**

  A.1 - Darcy' Law application   127
  A.2 - Sahara desertification   128
  A.3 - More on Sahara desertification   129
  A.4 - Murals of stone transportation   131
  A.5 - Average weight of the 2.3 million stones   132
  A.6 - Were there 2.3 Million stones in the Great Pyramid?   132
  A.7 - Volume of stone in the first seven courses   134
  A.8 - Pyramid dimensions used in calculations   135
  A.9 - To find the angle of the "arris" edge of the pyramid   135
  A.10 - Metric conversions   135
  A.11 - Stone/water density   135
  A.12 - Volume of water required to float the Great Pyramid   136
  A.13 - Water flow capacities of pipes   137
  A.14 - Artesian Wells and Flow Rates   137
  A.15 - Float/Lock Box/Water Stair size requirements   139
  A.16 - Bucket Brigade   141
  A.17 - Volume of water in the Enclosure Pond   141
  A.18 - Volumes of water and stone in the lock system   142
  A.19 - Volume of stone required for Phase 1 construction   142
  A.20 - Delivery rate of stones for the Phase 1 Construction   143
  A.21 - Delivery rate of stones for Phase 2 Construction   143
  A.22 - The Dynamics of the Water Stairs   144
  A.23 - Flow of the Nile River, Egypt   145
  A.24 - Flow of the Willamette River, Oregon   145
  A.25 - Notes on Tunnels   145
  A.26 - Notes on underground water causing problems   146
  A.27 - Copper Pipes   146
  A.28 - Estimate of Water Stairs Cycle Time   147

BIBLIOGRAPHY   **149**

AUTHORS' BIOGRAPHIES   **153**

  Samuel R. Sampson   153
  Michael N. Read   153

INTRODUCTION

"I think that only daring speculation can lead us further and not accumulation of facts"
Albert Einstein

Image 0.1 - The above image shows the edge or Arris angle of the Great Pyramid at ~42 degrees, more shallow than the face angle of ~52 degrees (See Appendix A.9)
Source: interoz.com/egypt/cheops.htm 09/06/2009

Floating Stones

After four thousand six hundred years, the story can now be told of how the Great Pyramid at Giza in Egypt was built. Our unique and startling interpretation of the existing evidence reveals how the ancient Egyptian architects and engineers used local water resources, knowledge of hydrological and maritime principles and their existing technologies to complete the pyramid in record time and with less manpower than previously imagined.

The purpose of this book is to present a rational theory of construction for the Great Pyramid based on the geological and architectural facts present at, or adjacent to, the construction site; many of these are still visible today. It is also based on historical data, documented knowledge, common sense and a great deal of circumstantial evidence. Paramount to our concept is our underlying assumption that the Egyptian people not only conceived of it, but also designed and constructed this magnificent monument.

Modern day experts seem to support the theory that the Ancient Egyptians delivered most of the stones from the quarry southwest of the pyramid, by virtue of a mega-ramp (see Chapter 5) erected on the pyramid's south façade; then hundreds of men (historically referred to as slaves) used ropes to haul the stones up the ramp to the pyramid level under construction. Other ramp

1

theories have also been advanced that suggest that the stones were dragged to their place in the rising pyramid construction using additional methods such as pulleys, levers and ramps combined in many proposed configurations. *They have yet to show convincingly how the giant monoliths were lifted to the upper levels of the pyramid* where the Queen's Chamber, the Grand Gallery and the King's Chamber are located, thus setting up a conflict between the acknowledged magnificence of the structure itself coexisting with their alleged primitive and labor-intensive methods of construction.

Our proposed construction method eliminates the need for slaves, ramps, ropes, levers, pulleys, wheels, sound waves, pumps, or technologies lost, supernatural or alien to the indigenous culture.

Egyptologists currently believe that the "Causeway", another ramp-like structure, was used for ritual and provided a pedestrian pathway from the Nile to the Pyramid. We conclude that the "Causeway" in fact was not for foot traffic at all, but was a series of water locks that allowed the stone-laden barges to float up directly from the River Nile to the pyramid and into a "moat-like" body of water (Enclosure Pond) contained between the pyramid and a wall constructed all around it (Enclosure Wall). This lock system made possible a two-phase stone delivery system powered by water. The first phase floated in all the large monoliths to be incorporated higher in the pyramid and all stones for the first seven courses as well. The second phase of delivery raised all remaining stones by means of small lock boxes (Water Stairs) to their respective levels and to the top of the pyramid where the "Pyramidian" was placed.

Great Pyramid Facts

The Great Pyramid at Giza, Egypt, is the only surviving monument of the original Seven Wonders of the Ancient World. Not only is it the sole survivor, but it was about two thousand years old when the second oldest wonder, the Hanging Gardens of Babylon, was built in about 600 BCE and then destroyed by earthquake five hundred years later. There was only a period of about sixty years when all seven ancient wonders existed concurrently and could have been visited by a traveler; that was in about 290 BCE.

Of the six Wonders that have passed into history, four were destroyed by earthquake and two by fire. How is it then that the Great Pyramid has been able to withstand the ravages of time? What is it about its design and construction that has made it so durable? No plans or descriptions of the

2

ancient building process have ever been found, so exactly how it was built is one of the pyramid mysteries that have challenged generations of explorers and intellectuals.

There exist a few ancient murals showing men with ropes dragging large statues (e.g. Djehutihotep's statue being moved in 12th Dynasty). There are other images of large stones being transported on boats and some pulled on sleds by oxen (see Appendix 4), but there is little ancient evidence of the Great Pyramid construction method itself.

The Greek historian Herodotus (circa 450 BCE) in his "Histories" wrote on pyramid construction as it was described to him by the Egyptian priests of his time, which was more than two thousand years after the pyramids were built. In one interesting chapter (see full quote Chapter 5) he states that *the causeway for the conveyance of the stones,* the leveling of the site and the underground chambers altogether took ten years to build, before the pyramid was started, and that this project was in his judgment a work not much inferior to the pyramid itself.

In another chapter (see full quote Chapter 8) Herodotus states that the pyramid was built in steps, battlement-wise, or altar-wise, *by machines made of short wooden planks,* which raised the stones up one level at a time and that there was either one machine at each level or the machine moved upwards one level at a time.

In a recent (October 2007) article *"Canal Linking Ancient Egyptian Quarry to Nile Found"* in the National Geographic News, Steve Stanek wrote that the ancient Egyptians were able to quarry the immense granite monoliths at Aswan, excavate a canal from the quarry to the Nile, load the monolith onto a barge, float it down the Nile and through another canal to a harbor in the vicinity of the Great Pyramid and hold it there for later use in the building process. *"What you have is very strong evidence that they may have loaded these stones in at the quarry...and as a result not dragging and hauling them over land,"* said Richard R. Parizek, a professor of geology at Penn State University (see full quote page 21)

Another tantalizing clue that boats and barges may have played a more prominent role in pyramid building is the presence of seven "boat pits" located around the Great Pyramid. These pits are carved into the solid limestone rock of the Giza Plateau. Five of them are boat-shaped and contain no boats. The two southernmost pits are rectangular shaped and were covered and sealed off air tight by huge limestone blocks. The most famous one contained a disassembled "boat kit" which was reassembled into the

3

Pharaoh's funerary boat and is on display in a specially constructed building at the Giza site (see Image 2.3A). The seventh pit has been peeked at and resealed.

The ancient Egyptians were master hydrologists due to their generations of experience in harnessing the life-giving waters of the Nile for their agricultural needs. They built dikes, canals and waterways controlled with sluice gates all along the Nile Valley to expand their arable farmland, minimize flood damage and to preserve water for use after the annual inundation had receded. So it is not surprising that they applied these same skills and resources to the construction of the greatest monument ever built by man...the Great Pyramid at Giza.

Whether you are an amateur historian or a serious student of Egyptology, we hope you enjoy following our journey of discovery. We invite you to "connect the dots" formed by the over thirty pieces of historical, physical and circumstantial evidence we cite in the following chapters, to see if you believe our theory "holds water".

Sam's Preface

In the spring of 2000, after having read *The Orion Mystery*, by Robert Bauval & Adrian Gilbert, I was relating what I had read to my friend and colleague, Mike Read. Mike and I were in the habit of meeting to discuss world events and common interests. At this particular meeting we were discussing the aspects of the Great Pyramid and Bauval's premise regarding the "Ventilation Shafts" when our conversation drifted to the sheer magnitude of the edifice and inevitably, to its construction.

As we pondered the greatness of our Fourth Dynasty counterparts (architects and engineers), I posed the rhetorical question to Mike, "Wow, what would you do if the Pharaoh walked into your office and said that he wanted you to design and construct a multi-use monument up on the Giza Plateau, that was required to be some 756 feet square at the base, approximately 481 feet tall, oriented to the four cardinal directions, culminating in a point at the top and completed in twenty years?"

When considered as a real commission, we began to theorize what steps would be required in order to effect such an undertaking. Again I put a question to Mike, "What would we have available to us in that location that we could work with to achieve such a charge." We stared at each other for a few moments then began to tick off the fundamental requirements. "Let's see" I said to Mike, "We know we have the *Desert*, which provides us with the stone; we have a lot of *Sky*, although we couldn't see much use of an unlimited amount of blue sky (unless you were talking about the Pharaoh's treasury!); Mike then said, *"People"*, which would provide us with an unlimited amount of manpower labor; and "what else" we mused? Suddenly, our collective light bulb lit up and as I was saying *"Water"*, Mike blurted out, *"the Nile."*

Having been born and raised on the southern Oregon coast, I was familiar with the latent power of water and had often watched the log trucks deliver enormous payloads of trees to the log ponds and rivers where longshoremen would raft them together for loading into the ocean-going ships. Through the use of tug boats, mechanical cranes and ingenuity, stevedores would pluck whole trees from the water and gracefully swing them into the holds of vessels for transport to far away worlds. The combination of power and grace set against the serenity of the placid waters of the bay made the whole operation seem other-worldly. With a few toots and whistles and little fanfare, the vessels full of logs would gently depart the docks with barely a ripple, and with a high tide to provide for the additional displacement now needed for the heavily-laden ship's cargo of wood, the vessels would disappear into the mist for ports unknown.

With the realization of the latent power of water firmly ensconced in my mind and the knowledge that transport of heavy payloads of stone on the River Nile was a common practice of the Ancient Egyptians, I knew that the answer to the construction of the pyramid lay partially in the maritime expertise of the people. Now the dilemma revolved around the ease of transport of heavy cargo on the river, juxtaposed to the problem of stacking enormous stones vertically on the surface of the desert floor, above the highest levels of the annual Nile inundation. The breakthrough came in the form of a naturally occurring phenomenon also present at the Giza Plateau and in the Sahara Desert since the beginning of time, the power present in the confined aquifers below, manifested by the artesian well.

A few months after our initial conversation, Mike and I had completed our basic premise that is presented in much greater detail in the following text. We then decided to test our idea against all that had been written, discovered or postulated concerning the construction of Khufu's pyramid *with the intent to disprove our theory*. As of this 2010 writing, we have been unable to disprove or in fact, find a single obstacle that cannot be solved or explained utilizing our theory. Instead, we have observed, much to our delight, that all current evidence, physical principles and even historical accounts are not at odds with our proposal, but actually support it better than any other proposal we have seen or heard of to date.

Samuel R. Sampson
Architect, Oregon, USA

Mike's Preface

Here is what I was thinking at that time in 2000 when Sam's first mention of Egypt brought the standard image into my mind's eye; pyramids in the background surrounded by miles of sand and people riding camels. I knew that there was a Nile river but knew little about it. However, having grown up in the south of England I did know something about megaliths. I had visited Stonehenge several times, first as a young teenager on a history class outing. I had touched the ancient stones with my hands and had tried climbing them. I also visited the Avesbury stone circles and the giant mound known as Silbury Hill, all on the South Downs. Those were the days when the sites were readily accessible. Now they are fenced off from the visiting crowds.

At that time there was a lot of speculation about how Stonehenge was built and what it really represented. It was known that the 'Bluestones' came from the Preseli Mountains in Wales where they were quarried and were probably taken along the coast on floats or barges and up the local rivers then dragged overland the last short distance to the site. I had several books on the probable significance of the site, which supported the theory that it was an astronomical observatory and predictor of seasons and heavenly events and no doubt a place of ritual.

Now with Sam's question I was forced to contemplate the building of The Great Pyramid at Giza, which was a whole new concept for me. Stonehenge is only a one-story building and the pyramids are like skyscrapers in contrast. How could the ancients have lifted such huge megaliths up so high with such accuracy in such a short time?

I was aware of the amazing power of moving water, even in small and seemingly insignificant quantities. I had visited the Weald and Downland Open Air Museum in Singleton, near Chichester in Sussex, England www.wealddown.co.uk. This amazing place is a reconstruction of an ancient English village comprised of buildings and artifacts rescued from the march of progress and assembled in one idyllic spot in the countryside. One of the exhibits there had impressed me considerably and it came to the forefront of my mind as I pondered Sam's question.

One has to realize that England is a pretty flat place and the rivers are just creeks by comparison to some of the world's rivers. Nevertheless the inhabitants at that time built impressive mill structures with very small heads of water. The reconstructed mill at Singleton was fed from a small duck pond about 100 ft across. A small stream fed the pond and a small windmill pumped water up from underground to augment the stream in the dry season. The mill was powered by a water wheel, which received its water from a small sluice impinging on the top of the wheel. The miller had control at his workstation with a number of knotted ropes nestled in wooden slots.

To start the wheel moving he would pull on a rope to open the sluice gate and let the water shoot out. The combination of the force and weight of the water would start the wheel turning. The miller would then reach for another rope, depending on what action he wanted. Some ropes were wound several turns around wooden rollers, which acted as clutches. With these the miller could hoist sacks of grain up the height of the mill into its attic storage. Other ropes connected to clutches that drove the grinding wheels. I watched in amazement as this small mill operated. There was no fuss, no smoke and almost no sound. The head of water was no more than a few feet and the amount of water used was very sparing. The ducks and geese never hurried and the whole operation was very environmentally sound. In the summer months volunteers, dressed in costumes of that period, operate the mill and put on a great show for the tourists.

So my thoughts were coming together around the power of water to move almost anything. I am also an avid kayaker and boater and have been through locks at many places in Europe and the Northwest. I know that a trickle of water can move a vessel as large as a building. I had also seen the power of the water rushing down the sides of Mt. St. Helens during the eruption of May 18, 1980. Buildings, bridges and heavy equipment were washed away like tinker toys in the deluge.

I knew that the solution to our problem had to rely on the power of moving water, and our task ahead was to learn more about the available water sources including the River Nile and its utilization in ancient Egypt.

Michael N. Read
Engineer/Appraiser, Oregon, USA

BACKGROUND – ANCIENT EGYPT

Tefnut Goddess of Water

Chapter 1 – River Nile and its Geology

In order to create the proper historical context for our theory about the construction of the Great Pyramid, it is appropriate to begin with a chapter on the River Nile and its geology. The powerful geological forces that created the Nile River also created a pressurized subterranean aquifer that made the pyramid construction possible. Without a solid comprehension of these facts, the theory presented herein may be difficult to understand. In this Chapter we will trace the source of the water pathway from the highlands of Ethiopia downhill through the subterranean aquifer, to the artesian well at the Giza Plateau.

The River Nile

The River Nile is unique among the world's river systems. Firstly, it is the longest river in the world; at 6,825 kilometers [1] the Nile is longer than the Amazon River, but the Amazon has more than 65 times the flow of water [2] discharging from it than does the Nile. That is because the Nile flows mostly through the African deserts, where there is little rainfall and where seepage into underground aquifers can occur. Perhaps the most unusual aspect of the Nile in Egypt is that it floods in the summertime, not in the winter when most areas of the world typically experience more rain. This fact always mystified the visitors to ancient Egypt and even the Egyptians of that time did not know the source of the Nile or the reason behind the flooding, even though it was the most important event in their agricultural calendar.

> *"I was particularly anxious to learn from them [the priests] why the Nile, at the commencement of the summer solstice, begins to rise and continues to increase for a hundred days – and why, as soon as that number is past, it forthwith retires and contracts its stream, continuing low during the whole of the winter until the summer solstice comes around again. On none of these points could I obtain any explanation from the inhabitants, though I made every inquiry, wishing to know what was commonly reported – they could neither tell me what special virtue the Nile has which makes it so opposite in its nature to all other streams ..." – Herodotus, The Histories, George Rawlinson translation, Chapter 19.*

Many expeditions attempted to find the source of the Nile even in relatively modern times. David Livingstone (1813-1873) the famous Scottish explorer failed to find the ultimate source and died trying. He found Lake Victoria, which he originally thought was the source of the Nile, and he named it after the Queen of England of that time. We now know that Lake Victoria is supplied by many other rivers, the largest of which is the River Kagera. Its tributary the Ruvubu has its headwaters in Burundi and this is now

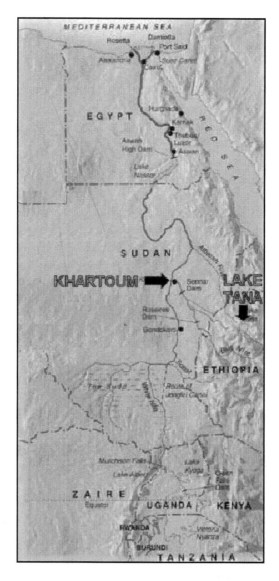

Image 1.1 - Reference Map of the Nile River
Source http://www.touregypt.net/magazine/mag05012001/nile3.jpg 09/06/2009
Authors added large type and arrows

considered to be the true source of the Nile (see bottom of Image 1.1 above).

On its way north, the river is first called the Victoria Nile, then the Albert Nile and then the White Nile until it reaches Khartoum in Sudan (ancient Nubia) where it is joined by the Blue Nile with its source at Lake Tana in the Ethiopian highlands. It is the Blue Nile together with the Atbara River, another Nile tributary further downstream, that creates the inundation or flooding of the subsequent Nile.

Lake Tana in Ethiopia

The Mountains of Ethiopia were formed approximately 700,000 years ago[3] by the volcanic upward thrusting of the north-central portion of the African continent, where the rock strata of the Sahara Desert, formerly a vast sea floor formed during the Cretaceous Period, were bent, buckled and warped upwards. The exposed limestone rock edges at the top of the mountain range (3,000 – 4,500 meters elevation) formed closed basins (Upper Rift, Omo, Awash and Assale)[4] totaling about 2,000 square kilometers where the rainfall produced a recharge zone to a vast subterranean aquifer that follows the slopes of the sub-strata downwards, north and west through Sudan and into Egypt west of the Nile. This subterranean aquifer also produced springs high up in the mountains. The most important set of springs is at Gishe Abay (2,744 meters elevation) and is the headwaters for Lake Tana and subsequently the Blue Nile.

Lake Tana (1,829 meters elevation)[5], is the source of the Blue Nile which travels some 1,750 kilometers in a clockwise circular route and drops 1,426 meters before reaching its confluence with the White Nile at Khartoum.

Image 1.2 The falls at Lake Tana, Ethiopia
Source: www.natytoursethiopia.com.et/Tana.htm 09/06/2009

From Khartoum the combined River Nile makes its serpentine way through the expansive desert, collecting its last tributary, the Atbara River, before passing over the five original cataracts and entering its final channel that begins at the location of the present Aswan Dam just upstream from the ancient site of Elephantine Island. The Nile's final journey to the Mediterranean Sea is approximately 1000 kilometers (about 620 miles). The visible River Nile is the above-ground manifestation of an even greater water source underground (see Nubian Aquifer, below).

Nile Flow Rate

The Annual Nile Flow chart (Image 1.3) shows how the White Nile contributes a relatively small but fairly consistent amount of water to the overall Nile throughout the year, with a slightly larger amount during the months of October - December. The Blue Nile is by far the greatest contributor to the inundation period which runs from August through October. The flow rates in the chart are confirmed in Dr. Rushdi Said's book "The River Nile: Geology, Hydrology and Utilization", page 110, where a detailed table shows the average monthly flow rates. They convert to an average flow of roughly 230 million cubic meters per day with the peak flow occurring in August/September producing about 700 million cubic meters per day.

Prior to the existence of the Aswan Dam, the effect of this annual inundation was like a tidal flow, with the high tide lasting about 100 days through August, September, October and a few days of November. The high water level reached to almost 60 meters Above Mean Sea Level (AMSL), coincidentally a height that extends almost to the base of the Great Pyramid. Then, as the inundation receded during the next nine months of the year, the shoreline moved incrementally closer to the lowest known Nile level of about 20 meters AMSL.

That represented a seasonal fluctuation in water levels of approximately 40 meters. In addition to the phenomenal amount of water being discharged by the Nile above ground, the underground aquifer as a part of the system, greatly exceeded in volume that of the surface water.

Unfortunately we could find no information on volume or flow for the underground aquifer. However, the following article extract does confirm its existence and general magnitude.

14

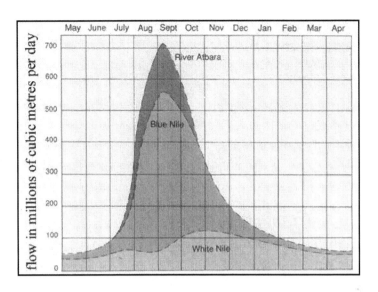

Image 1.3 Annual Nile Flow
Source: www.mbarron.net/Nile/flowrate.jpg 09/06/2009

Nubian Aquifer

...Under the Sahara lie three major aquifers, strata of saturated sandstones and limestones that hold water in their pores like a wet sponge. The easternmost of these, extending over two million square kilometers, underlies all of Egypt west of the Nile, all of eastern Libya, and much of northern Chad and Sudan, and contains 375,000 cubic kilometers of water—the equivalent of 3750 years of Nile River flow. It is called the Nubian Sandstone Aquifer System ...

Source: Saudi Aramco World Jan/Feb 2007 Volume 58, Number 1. Article "Seas Beneath the Sands" by Louis Werner and Kevin Bubriske.

http://www.saudiaramcoworld.com/issue/200701/seas.beneath.the.sands.ht
m   9/06/2009

Artesian Wells

Image 1.4 shows how an upturned permeable rock stratum creates a recharge zone where the water sinking underground becomes an aquifer which flows downhill under pressure from the water above contained between two impermeable layers. A well can be drilled down through the upper layer and the water will rise up to a level known as the "potentiometric height". If a well exists below this height the result is known as an artesian well. Such

15

flowing wells in the desert are known as oases, which were well known and understood in Ancient Egypt.[6]

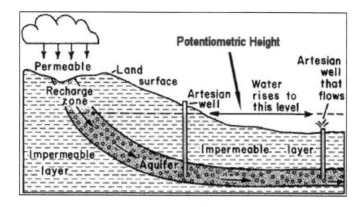

Image 1.4 - Artesian Well. Source: USGS Image

If a flowing artesian well is confined above grade it will rise to that potentiometric height. Variables such as the elevation of the recharge zone, the elevation at the well and the horizontal distance between them factor into the subsequent flow. Also, the amount of water discharge through such a well depends on the permeability and cross sectional area of the porous rock stratum. In 1856, following the work of Blaise Pascal, the French hydrologist Henry Darcy published an equation that formed the relationship between these variables of water flow through a porous medium. We have developed Darcy's Law formula a little further in Appendix A.1, to show that the cross sectional area of permeable rock stratum to produce the flow needed for our theory is well within reason.

The fundamental principle of the confined aquifer is well illustrated by the common garden hose. If a hose is filled with water, and one end is held higher than the other, water will run out of the hose at the lower end propelled by the weight of the water above it. Water will continue to issue from the hose until the water level at both ends is equal (or the hose is empty), whereupon the water will cease to flow.

Magnitudes of flow for the artesian aquifer at the Giza Plateau during the Fourth Dynasty were of course not recorded. However, we have evaluated the pressure levels and flow rates for typical artesian wells in Appendix A.14.

16

Nile Source Elevations

Image 1.5 shows the various water source locations important to the Nile with their relative elevations and distances from the Mediterranean Sea. The chart exaggerates the scale of the elevations with respect to distance but demonstrates the huge potential for underground water pressure at the Giza location. The Giza Plateau is at 60 meters AMSL whereas the top of the Great Pyramid is at 200 meters AMSL.

Referring back to Image 1.4, the artesian well, imagine the recharge zone being at the height of Mt. Gishe and the confined aquifer descending underground from that height down past Khartoum and ultimately to Giza; the cross-section illustrates the great potential for a flowing artesian well at the Giza location.

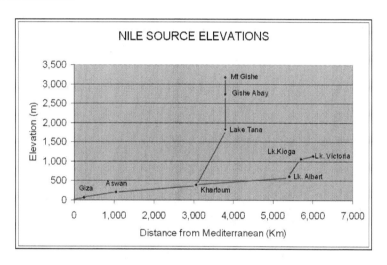

Image 1.5 Nile Source Elevations – Source: The Authors

Our theory holds that, up to the time of the building of the Giza Pyramids, the climate was much wetter, particularly in the Ethiopian Highlands and the potentiometric height at the Giza Plateau was such that the natural artesian flow could be contained within the structure of the pyramid and had the potential to reach the topmost courses of the pyramid at about 200 meters AMSL

Sahara Desertification

Also, during this ancient time, the climate was in transition to a more arid one, which according to climate researchers was partially caused by a change

17

in the Earth's orbit (Appendix A.2). This gradual drying, referred to as 'Sahara Desertification', was well underway during the reigns of the Pharaohs Khufu and Khafre (Appendix A.3) and in addition to creating reduced agricultural production it drastically reduced the pressure and availability of the underground aquifer and reduced its accompanying potentiometric height. It is our belief that this loss of pressure, in addition to the ecological, financial and political ramifications of the drier climate, was the primary reason for the end of the building of the large stone pyramids.

> *'When the Nile overflows, the country is converted into a sea, and nothing appears but the cities, which look like the islands in the Aegean.'* Herodotus – The Histories, Chapter 97 Page 171

1. Said, Rushdi. *The River Nile: Geology, Hydrology and Utilization.* New York: Permagon Press, 1994. p. 9.
2. Said, Table on p. 9.
3. Said, p. 4.
4. Said, Fig. 1.10 p. 23
5. Said, p. 26.
6. Thurston, Harry. *Secrets of the Sands.* Doubleday Canada, 2003, pages 180-181.

Chapter 2 – Resources and Skills

In this Chapter, we will cover a wide range of information about Ancient Egypt at the time the pyramids were built to illustrate how workmen, architects and engineers of the era regularly employed all of the skills and techniques required by our theory. In fact, these activities were in such commonplace use that our proposed explanation of pyramid construction would almost inevitably have been drawn from and based on the experience of the architects of that age and the methods they commonly used.

Agriculture

The Egyptians, due to their efforts at understanding and channeling water from the annual flooding of the Nile for the purposes of agriculture, as pyramid builders, developed many complex hydrological techniques. The following will illustrate the breadth of their agricultural activities and how their water management needs educated them in the ways of water.

The following passage was written about 450 BCE (2,110 years after the Great Pyramid was built) and discussed the Egyptian farmers in the Nile Delta region of Egypt.

> *"At present it must be confessed, they obtain the fruits of the field with less trouble than any other people in the world, the rest of the Egyptians included, since they have no need to break up the ground with the plough, not to use the hoe, nor to do any of the work, which the rest of mankind find necessary if they are to get a crop; but the husbandman waits till the river has of its own accord spread itself over the fields and withdrawn again to its bed, and then sows his plot of ground, and after sowing turns his swine into it – the swine tread the corn – after which he has only to await the harvest." Herodotus - The Histories, Chapter 14*

The above statement over simplifies the nature of farming in all of Egypt because ploughs pulled by oxen and hand tools such as the hoe were used to break up the earth in preparation for seeding. But it was true that the River Nile was unique in its ability to replenish the soil with silt, wash away the harmful salts and produce a crop with less preparation than other places in the ancient world.

In order to provide for an expanding population afforded by the riches of the Nile valley, the Egyptian people became the world's greatest hydrologists, creating vast new acreage of arable farmland that was previously limited to the narrow banks of the Nile's annual inundation. The Egyptians became adept at irrigation farming, diverting water long distances and storing it to provide for additional irrigation. The control over these waterways was achieved using sluice gates such as reed-matted or hide-covered gates or wooden slats, which were kept under constant supervision by trained crews. Such a system required vigilance, maintenance and community wide coordination.

The Faiyum, a naturally occurring basin south and west of Giza, was in early dynastic times a well-stocked wetland, replenished by the annual inundation, but possibly in part due to the faults in the limestone rock stratum of the desert floor allowing subterranean water to seep to the surface creating that most alluring of desert charms, the oasis. The other naturally-occurring oases, of which there were several settled by the early Egyptians, by their presence revealed an additional water source available to them, located underground.

Boats and Transportation

Agriculture was not the only activity that added to the Egyptian's ability to employ water. As is well understood, some stones of the pyramids were transported a great distance from a few quarries to the building site, and were generally believed to have been moved by barges on the Nile. We believe that barges were also used in the construction process itself. Though this may seem quite a leap, we will make a solid case for this hypothesis. But to begin, we will lay a foundation for the maritime skills that existed in Egypt at the time.

The Egyptians developed the world's greatest navy[1], an odd fact when you consider that in most people's mind's eye, the Egyptians were a desert people. However, the Nile changed all that and dictated that the locals deal with its rising and receding volumes both seasonally and on a daily basis. They used the Nile's power to transport goods, not just by floating barges downriver, but also upriver, thanks to the ubiquitous winds that swept off the Mediterranean Sea and southwards up the Nile. This natural phenomenon was the overriding factor that enabled the Egyptian navy to develop into the formidable force that it became; through use of the sail, they learned to master the Nile in both directions.

This later allowed them to proceed on many expeditions throughout the eastern Mediterranean, not the least of which was their acquisition of the highly prized Cedar trees at Byblos in ancient Phoenicia, (now Lebanon) and to protect the mouth of the Nile from the "Sea Peoples" and other potential invaders. This maritime expertise, coupled with their emerging stevedore and longshoreman knowledge and capabilities provided the technology needed to move great payloads up, down and across the Nile and proved to be indispensable during the construction of the country's greatest monuments.

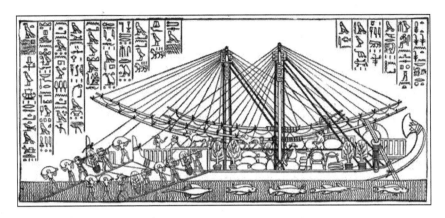

Image 2.1: Large Nile river boat being loaded
Source: http://karenswhimsy.com/public-domain-images/ 02/23/2010

It has long been established the Egyptians used large boats and barges to move heavy loads, including large monoliths such as obelisks, along the River Nile. They also constructed artificial harbors close to the pyramids to hold water and building materials in readiness for the construction. A recent (October 2007) article "Canal Linking Ancient Egyptian Quarry to Nile Found" in the National Geographic News, Steve Stanek wrote:

> *"Experts have discovered a canal at an Aswan rock quarry that they believe was used to help float some of ancient Egypt's largest stone monuments to the Nile River. It has long been suspected that ancient workers moved the massive artifacts directly to their final destinations over waterways. Ancient artwork shows Egyptians using boats or barges to move large monuments like obelisks and statues, and canals have also been discovered at the Giza pyramids and the Luxor Temple. But the newfound canal, which has since been filled in, is the first proof discovered at the granite quarries in Aswan. Almost all obelisks, including those at the Luxor and Karnak Temples, were originally hewn in the Aswan area. "What you have is very strong evidence that they may have loaded these stones in at the quarry ... and as a result not dragging and hauling them over land,"*

21

said Richard R. Parizek, a professor of geology at Penn State University who led the scientific tests confirming the canal's existence. "It eliminates that land connection."

Source: http://touregypt.net/teblog/egyptologynews/?p=3068 09/06/2009

The above article establishes that the ancient Egyptians were skillful enough to quarry immense granite monoliths at Aswan, excavate a canal from the quarry to the Nile, load a monolith onto a barge, float it down the Nile and into a harbor in the vicinity of the Great Pyramid, then hold it there for later incorporation in the building. It seems likely that they would keep these large stones on their barges for as long as possible and extend the reach of the waterway as opposed to unloading the barge and dragging the stone over land. See Appendix A.4 for additional images of stone transportation.

Boat Construction

The basic method of Egyptian boat building of the time was borrowed by the pyramid builders to construct the wooden locks utilized in the construction of the pyramid. This is important since both the capability of the craftsmen and the adapted techniques utilized in the construction of the wooden locks, show how such processes were well within the grasp of the builders and also serves to lay the groundwork for supporting the archaeological evidence at the site of the pyramid.

The River Nile became the major transportation highway but its large width and annual inundation did not allow bridges to be built and this gave rise to many small boats acting as ferryboats carrying people and goods from one side to the other. These early small craft were papyrus rafts, similar to those shown in Image 2.2, carrying one or two people and baggage. They gradually became larger and more sophisticated and developed into wooden boats that looked remarkably similar in design.

Image 2.2 Papyrus boats on modern day Lake Tana in Ethiopia.
Source: http://www.travelswithsheila.com/the_blue_nile_falls_north_ethi.html 09/06/2009

The process of Sahara desertification mentioned in Chapter 1 had begun in the equatorial highlands and resulted in lower Nile levels, which began in the First Dynasty (3,100 BCE) and was fully involved by the end of the Fourth Dynasty[2] (2,600 BCE), which limited the availability of trees such as oak and pine for boat building in the age of the pyramids. Consequently the domestic wood supply was limited, mostly low quality and could only be cut into short planks. Trees such as Acacia, Carob, Juniper and other local woods were used. This required that they make the shells of their boats almost like a patchwork quilt of short planks held adjacent by mortis and tenon joints and secured by ropes drawn through V-shaped holes carved into the planks. The seams were sealed with reeds and held in place with rounded battens. There was no wooden keel or wooden ribs to form the skeleton of the boat, which was given shape by attaching wooden cross pieces and pulling up the ends of the boat, using the mast as a support.

Further information on ancient Egyptian boats can be found at the following:

Source: http://nefertiti.iwebland.com/timelines/topics/index.html.

Boats and Boat Pits

Now that we have seen that the technology existed for large scale use of the boats and barges at the time of construction of the pyramids, let's examine some of the archaeological evidence that supports the use of boats at the construction site.

There are seven boat pits around the Great Pyramid site. Five of them are boat shaped open pits carved out of the limestone bedrock and are empty (see Image 2.4 below). The other two are rectangular shaped pits covered with large stone lintels (see Image 2.3B, below). All pits are very large. The southern pit on the east side is 51.5 meters long, seven meters wide at its midpoint and eight meters deep.

Images 2.3A The boat and 2.3B the rectangular boat pit (see Source below).

The two southern pits were discovered in 1954 by the young Egyptian architect and archaeologist Kamal el-Mallakh and inspector Zaki Nur. They are rectangular pits with disassembled boats (boat kits) placed in them and roofed over with large monoliths. The most famous of these has been reassembled under the supervision of Ahmed Youssef Mustafa, the master restorer. It is now displayed in a specially designed building at the Giza site. Its assembled length is 43.3 meters (142 feet) long and made of Lebanese cedar wood and some acacia. Its displacement was 45 tons. The maximum draft is 1.48 meters (5 feet). It is 5.9 meters wide.

Source: http://www.touregypt.net/featurestories/greatpyramid5.htm 11/15/2009

The assembled boat is too large to fit in its rectangular pit in the assembled state. Its design with oars, rudder and cabin appears to have been made for human travel, perhaps for the final journey of the Pharaoh Khufu to his Valley Temple; therefore his boat became part of the archived funerary offerings so typical of the Egyptian culture.

Image 2.4 One of five empty boat-shaped pits.
Source: http://www.touregypt.net/featurestories/greatpyramid5.htm 11/15/2009

On the other hand, the five open boat pits were empty except for a few scraps of wood and other debris. Nobody really knows what they represent. However, since the pits themselves were boat-shaped, even empty, their very presence adjacent to the Great Pyramid indicates that boats were venerated objects. If so, this makes the connection between the maritime expertise of the Ancient Egyptians and the construction of the monument.

Sadd-Al-Kafara Dam

A further indication that water played a significant role in early pyramid construction is provided by the existence of the remains of the Sadd-Al-Kafara Dam. Although the Egyptians mostly remained being stewards of their environment, they occasionally attempted to become masters of their universe, pushing the envelope beyond their capabilities. One such occasion was the construction of the Sadd-Al-Kafara dam, which they built adjacent to the Giza Plateau, upriver from Cairo approximately 25 kilometers, just east of Helwan, between 2,686 and 2498 BCE, about the time of the Great Pyramid's construction.

Discovered in 1885 by a German archaeologist, G. Schweinfurth, this was the world's first known attempt to construct a stone dam across a river

25

anywhere in the world and Sadd-Al-Kafara was to extend the full distance across the Wadi Al-Garawi damming its river, possibly to provide flood control, drinking water, or a harbor for workers at the alabaster quarry located approximately 4 kilometers east; the harbor may also have been intended as a holding pond for stockpiled stones on barges awaiting delivery to the Great Pyramid.

This rubble dam was faced and fitted with roughly cut limestone blocks set in stepped courses and was approximately 14 meters high, 113 meters along the crest, with the sloping outer faces approximately 13 meters wide at the top and 24 meters wide at the base. Apparently, the Ancient Egyptians did not use mortar to seal the stone facing, with the result that the central section of the dam failed, probably due to percolation of water through and under the dam; it is not known whether a spillway was provided to allow excess water to pass safely over the top. In all likelihood, none was provided and overspill from the full dam probably caused erosion on the downstream side, leading to its catastrophic failure and possibly sending a wall of water down the Nile that would have wiped out small settlements of population in its path all the way to the Mediterranean.

(Source: http://weekly.ahram.org.eg/2004/708/he1.htm -11/31/2010).

The Egyptians never made another attempt to dam an entire river (until the early 1900's when the first Aswan dam was built), resorting instead to creating smaller bays, harbors and quays, in connection with other existing wadis (gullies) that drained periodic flashfloods and lie adjacent to the main flow of the river.

Wells and Rock Drilling

The Egyptians ability to tunnel through rock is evidenced in all the pyramids from the 3rd Dynasty Step Pyramid of Djoser at Saqqara to the much smaller pyramids all the way through to the 12th dynasty. Our theory, in part, suggests that the pyramid builders drilled down below the construction site to tap the natural pressurized artesian water underground.

It is well established that the Egyptians used drills to cut holes in wood and stone since the early dynastic period. They used bow drills to hollow out stone vases and to cut beads for jewelry. Although no copper drill barrels have been found, the results of their use is evident from the remaining cores, such as the one depicted in Image 2.5 below. They range is size from 0.6 cm to 75 cm in diameter. The Great Pyramid at Giza has a Well/Grotto and a

Subterranean Chamber with a "pit"; many other large stone pyramids also have chambers at or below grade. They are often referred to as tombs, catacombs or burial chambers but no Pharaohs have been found buried therein. It could be that ancient robbers had long ago plundered all the tombs and removed the buried Kings and their treasure. It is our belief that the tunnel (Descending Corridor) at the Great Pyramid was excavated to reach the underlying permeable rock strata that contained artesian water under pressure.

Water under the Giza Plateau

Clearly, today, there is not enough water pressure at the site of the pyramid to enable construction as we propose. But in ancient times, the climate of the Nile Valley was quite different.

Image 2.5 Granite Core form Tubular Drill Hole
Source:
http://www.geocities.com/unforbidden geology/ancient egyptian copper coring drills.html
09/06/2009

Further indications of the Egyptians' familiarity with subterranean excavations are provided by Andrew Collins in his book *"Beneath the Pyramids – Egypt's Greatest Secret Uncovered" (2009)*, in which he describes an enormous system of caves and tunnels under the Giza Plateau.

Collins claims to have found the lost underworld of the pharaohs after reading the forgotten memoirs of the 19th century diplomat and explorer Henry Salt (1780-1827) and his Italian colleague Giovanni Battista Caviglia (1770-1845).

The book describes, and has color photos, that show clearly a combination of natural caves and improved spaces in the limestone substrata, many of which appear to be eroded by the passage of underground water. They appear similar to the Subterranean Chamber under the Great Pyramid which is described in more detail in Chapter 4.

Collins' book also describes an existing well named Bir-es-Samman[3] located in a modern Islamic cemetery just 250 yards south of the Sphinx, on the Giza Plateau.

This book provides additional support for our theory that there was plentiful underground water beneath the Giza Plateau in ancient times.

The Quarries

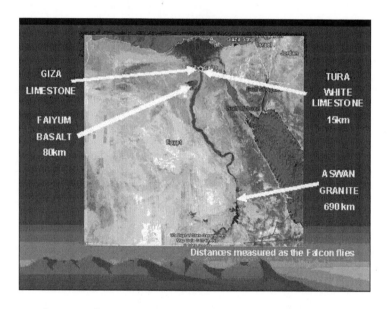

Image 2.6 Quarry locations: Source the Authors and Google Earth

In this section we will address the various locations throughout Egypt from which the Egyptians obtained the building materials that were incorporated within the Great Pyramid. Since the quarries were in some cases far flung from the Giza Plateau, their use of the River Nile as their transportation highway for materials delivery further connects their maritime expertise and natural resources with the construction site.

Before delving into the details of our theory, it is important to first consider the phenomenal amount of stone incorporated within the monument (see Appendix A.5) and to realize that work must have begun in the quarries as soon as the decision was made to utilize certain types of stone in the construction. Work required that the stones first be freed from the live rock at the locations containing the rock deemed to be the most appropriate for the job. That meant that work began simultaneously at not less than three sites, and perhaps as many as five. Recent work by the American Egyptologist Dr. Mark Lehner, has earmarked the quarry that lies just southwest of the Great Pyramid, within a few hundred meters of the site, for providing most of the limestone core blocks used within the monument.

It appears that the gleaming white limestone casing stones were floated across the Nile River, from the quarries of Tura and Maasara about 15 kilometers east of Giza. The large granite monoliths used in the interior of the King's Chamber appear to have been supplied by the quarries at Aswan, several hundred kilometers (about 430-miles as the falcon flies) up the River Nile. It has recently been determined that much of the basalt used in ancient Egyptian temple construction came from an Oligocene flow located at the northern edge of the Faiyum Oasis, a naturally-occurring lake about 80 kilometers southwest of the Giza Plateau, that was also delivered by water when the inundation made its annual connection to the Nile possible.

As a function of the volume of the pyramid, it has been estimated approximately 2.3 million blocks weighing an average of 2.5 tons each were needed. In reality, the actual number of stones that were needed is indeterminate. According to Sir William Matthew Flinders Petrie (1853-1942), noted English Egyptologist known as the "Father of Egyptian Archaeology, the individual course measurements varied considerably. See Appendices A.5 and A.6, where our estimates conclude that 2.3 million stones would average closer to 2.9 tons each and that the number of stones is indeterminate, as Petrie concluded. Coursework thickness varied layer to layer more than likely due to the particular rock formation that was being quarried and delivered to the jobsite at any point in time.

Image 2.7 – Unfinished Obelisk at Aswan Quarry
Source: lexicorient.com/egypt/aswan10.htm 5/11/10

Gypsum

As a final comment regarding the resources available to the Ancient Egyptians, gypsum is available in great quantities in the Sahara Desert and was probably utilized as one of the components in the fine thin mortar between the pyramid blocks, for ease of placement and for strengthening the bond between blocks.

Wet gypsum is extremely slippery and probably facilitated the movement of the large blocks on the pyramid platform, allowing each block on its sledge to be ferried along to its particular destination with ease and aplomb, akin to the latter day "skid roads", famous in the American northwest logging industry and elsewhere worldwide.

Gypsum crusts can also be associated with playas, and these are apt to be soft, easily broken, and a major source of dust. When wetted after a rain, these surfaces are very slippery and gooey.

Source:http://www.agc.army.mil/research/products/desert_guide/lsmsheet/lsgyp.htm 06/01/2010

---

1. Gilbert, Gregory "Ancient Egyptian Sea Power" Chapter 6.
2. Said, Rushdi. "The River Nile: Geology, Hydrology and Utilization" Part II, Chart, page 137.
3. Collins, Andrew "Beneath the Pyramids" Chapter 9 http://www.andrewcollins.com

PHASE 1 CONSTRUCTION

Tefnut Goddess of Water

Lower Pyramid Elements

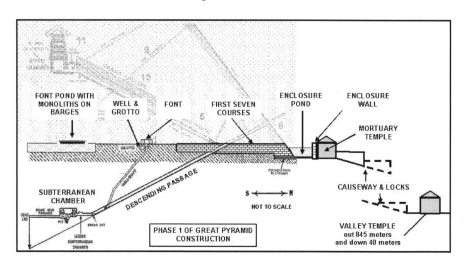

Image 3.0: Lower pyramid elements north-south cross section.
Causeway and locks shown for illustration are actually located on the east façade. Source: The Authors

A concise accounting and understanding of the construction process requires the reader to have some knowledge of the physical features of the site and structure. The elements listed below had to be completed first in order to facilitate the pyramid construction below the eighth course. Many of these activities were pursued concurrently and each element is described in detail in the following Chapters 3 and 4.

Well and Grotto	A well dug in the rock before the pyramid was built
Descending Corridor	A corridor dug to reach the subterranean aquifer
Subterranean Chamber	Excavated to collect subterranean water
Font	Water flowing to the surface from the subterranean aquifer
Font Pond	A pond created to float all the monoliths on barges
Enclosure Wall	Wall built all around the pyramid base 10 meters distant
Enclosure Pond	Pond within the Enclosure Wall to float stones on barges
Mortuary Temple	Few remains of the upper lock later converted to temple
Causeway and Locks	Proposed series of locks from pyramid to Nile River
Valley Temple	No remains of proposed lower lock later converted to temple
First Seven Courses	First seven layers of stones up to height of Enclosure Wall

Chapter 3 – Site Selection, Survey and Preparation

In this Chapter, we will discuss the various reasons the Giza Plateau was chosen for the site for the Great Pyramid. Image 3.1 is a topographical map of the Giza Plateau showing, from right to left, the Great Pyramid of Khufu, Khafre's pyramid and the smaller Red Pyramid of Mycerinus. The "Causeways" are shown as dark lines and the Causeway of the Great Pyramid is shown as it might have been since there are few remains to determine the actual configuration or location. For reference, the Sphinx is located at the lower center adjacent and north of the end of Khafre's Causeway and Valley Temple.

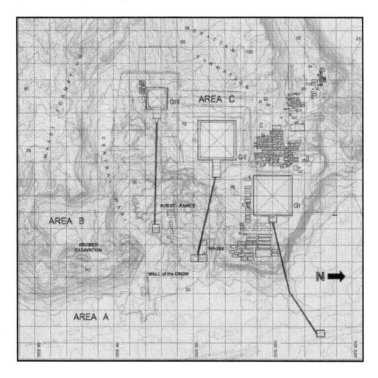

Image 3.1 - Giza Plateau showing three pyramids and causeway positions.
Source: http://www.aeraweb.org/khufu_quarry.asp 8/05/2009

Site Selection

Due to a possible previous disaster of the pyramid at Dashur, the ancient Egyptians must have been intent on properly locating the Great Pyramid on solid ground. The Bent Pyramid at Dashur, built by Senefru 2613-2589

33

BCE, underwent a radical design change while under construction (as theorized by many Egyptologists) due to a shifting foundation that gave way to the massive loads imposed upon a sand-founded site. Cracks, visible in the lowest coursework, allegedly prompted the designers to modify the steep slope of 54° 27', to a much shallower 43° 22', thereby greatly reducing the volume of stones needed to finish the edifice, resulting in a smaller load to be superimposed on the compromised pyramid from that point forward. Neither of these angles were to be incorporated in the Great Pyramid, nor was the foundation of shifting sands.

The site chosen for the Great Pyramid was the result of a great many considerations, a "rock solid" foundation being among the most important. The site is situated at the end of a limestone outcropping that had emerged from the seabed approximately 700,000 years ago to become the Moqattam and Maadi formations at Giza, thus influencing the course of the Nile since that time. Geologically speaking, the Nile Valley marks the end of the Sahara Desert's eastern margin and separates it from the Sinai Peninsula, to the east. The large limestone strata under the site run to great depths and are interspersed by deposits of sand and gravel, all of which are excellent upon which to found a structure of an exceedingly heavy nature. The Great Pyramid's existence today, more than four thousand five hundred years later, testifies to the wisdom of the builder's decision to locate it there.

Its location, immediately adjacent to the highest level of the Nile's annual inundation was also important. Reportedly, the Nile River approached the level of the bottom of the Great Pyramid. If so, this facilitated the maritime delivery of the stones obtained from the various quarries.

Another consideration was the site's proximity to an adequate source of stone suitable for the planned construction. The shorter the distance to the construction site, the less work and time was needed to deliver the payload. The Giza Plateau area became the local quarry that provided the bulk of the limestone core blocks incorporated within the pyramid.

A value-added feature of the site included a naturally-occurring outcrop of limestone that would be retained to project up into the core area of the pyramid. This provided three additional dividends: 1) incorporating the outcrop meant that superfluous rock would not have to be excavated and removed, 2) fewer limestone blocks would need to be quarried and transported to the site, saving considerable resources during construction and, 3) allowing the outcrop to remain also provided a natural keystone with which to structurally reinforce the entire pyramid, thereby increasing its resistance to earthquakes and the destructive forces of time.

The site was also close to Memphis, the early capital of the northern kingdom and was also close to the royal residence known as White Wall. This proximity would have facilitated the Pharaoh and his court in monitoring the progress of this most ambitious of governmental projects, as it arose from the Giza Plateau. There was no doubt continual interaction of the Pharaoh with his Vizier, (reportedly Hemiunu) during the course of construction and their proximity to the site allowed decisions and directions to be passed on a timely basis to the Vizier for dissemination to his superintendents.

One of the side benefits of building the pyramid in the first place, according to Peter Tompkins, author of *Secrets of the Great Pyramid (1971)*, was to provide a benchmark for fairly and accurately re-staking out the lot lines of farmland property which had been obscured by the flood, as soon as the annual inundation had receded, so that the farmers could get busy producing the nation's grain reserves and taxation could be meted out on a rational basis relative to how much farmland each farmer was responsible for. It is generally agreed among Egyptologists, that the topmost stone, the Pyramidian, was sheathed in gold or electrum. At approximately 48-stories above the desert floor, at noon, with Saharan sun beating down on it, the reflection of the Pyramidian could be seen literally, for tens of miles. A surveyor with the requisite plumb line and keen eyesight could easily, quickly and accurately re-establish the property lines to facilitate a prompt resumption of farming activities and apportionment of taxes.

Also in Tompkins' book, Livio Stecchini provides an illuminating prologue regarding the first established measurement and quantity systems and goes on to say that the second and third Giza pyramids could have facilitated long-distance surveying further, allowing the field surveyor to triangulate his position in the Egyptian countryside with great accuracy from year to year. The fact that the smallest pyramid was finished in red granite, visually aided a surveyor in ensuring he was viewing both Khufu's and Khafre's pyramids in their correct relative positions, thereby making the determinations of direction easier and exacting.

In order to incorporate all the components of the design, the chosen site had to be big and flat. The size of the site, approximately 13 acres for the footprint of the pyramid alone, had additionally to accommodate the numerous accessory outbuildings located nearby.

One other site feature was, in our opinion, of greater importance to the timely success of this project than any other; the presence of a subterranean aquifer directly below the pyramid. We will explain its significance in Chapter 4.

Artesian Well

It is our belief that the Ancient Egyptian architects and engineers recognized that the source of water flowing out of the artesian well, referred to above and in Chapter 1, could be used to create a head of water to power the system they had planned to use, to float the stones up to the pyramid construction site. They had to build a reservoir of water sufficient to operate a series of locks from the pyramid's east side, following the most shallow slope of the topography down to the bank of the Nile at its lowest level, so that delivery of stones could be a year-round operation. We believe they envisaged a wall all around the pyramid built up to the height of the well-head to contain sufficient water to create this reservoir. This wall is known as the Enclosure Wall and the water it retained we have named the Enclosure Pond. In Chapter 7 we discuss the volume of the Enclosure Pond, how long it would take to fill up, and how successfully it could contribute to the operation of the lock system.

Image 3.2 Photograph of the Vendome Well, Sulphur, Oklahoma
Source: http://www.okgenweb.org/~okmurray/Murray/images/vendome/'

As an example of the power inherent in artesian wells, the photo in Image 3.2 above shows the Vendome Well, located in Sulphur, Oklahoma, USA. When drilled in 1922, the well issued forth 3,500 gallons per minute, making it, at that time, the largest artesian well in the world; it shot water up into the air 28 feet!

Image 3.3 Photograph of the Vendome Well, Sulphur, Oklahoma
Source: http://www.okgenweb.org/~okmurray/Murray/images/vendome/'

The photo in Image 3.3 shows the Vendome Well as it appears today, issuing forth a reduced flow of approximately 500 gallons per minute, significantly more than the 22 cu. ft. per minute, or 164 gallons per minute (see Appendix 12) required to build the pyramid with water power.

See Appendix A.14 for more information on typical artesian wells and flow rates

Site Survey

Once the site was selected, an enormous amount of work was required to prepare the site, including the adjacent mobilization areas, prior to the delivery of the stones. Once the basic dimensions of the plan were known, the design could be laid out on the site to verify its ability to incorporate all components.

Much has been written about the methods the Ancient Egyptians utilized to obtain a perfect alignment with the four cardinal directions. Suffice it to say, that by plotting the daily rise and fall of the heavenly bodies on the horizons and bisecting their arc, they were able to align the building with true north.

Their observation and use of the pathways of the sun and the stars resulted in an extremely accurate layout, varying only a few centimeters over the 230 meters (756-feet) length of the sides of the Great Pyramid, good enough for government work now, unbelievably good then.

Site Leveling

After removal of the excess rock not used as a part of the central keystone, it has been suggested that the leveling (or terracing) of the site was accomplished by the stone masons who cut a grid pattern of troughs in the bedrock, flooding them with water to reveal the uneven ridges, which were then chipped and spalled away, ultimately leaving remarkably flat and uniform platforms upon which to found the massive weight of the imported stones. This flooding and leveling process was most likely aided by building mud brick walls at the perimeter of, or around portions of the pyramid site area, to retain the water; later these temporary walls would be replaced by a single permanent stone wall around the entire pyramid, known as the Enclosure Wall.

We know from survey information that the majority of the pyramid perimeter platform was leveled at about sixty meters AMSL except for that portion of the original rock mound that was left in place to form the central keystone. It makes good sense that the cornerstones in their square sockets were laid first to give the whole pyramid its cardinal orientation. This would have represented an immoveable two-dimensional framework from which to start. Upon these cornerstones the right-angled corner casing stones must have been placed to form the primal three-dimensional shape that infers the virtual finished pyramid. The face angle of the pyramid is equivalent to a slope of about 15 in 12 or ~52 degrees.

The first few layers of core blocks were chosen to be among the largest stones used and their corresponding casing stones were selected to be the same height. Limestone layers tend to be uniform over large quarry areas with each layer being slightly different due to the seabed formation eons ago. With the first and largest layer being 58 inches thick, the perimeter area of the footprint was leveled between the corner stones and then cut back into the mound to a depth of 58 inches to accommodate the first layer, which may have been only a few stones deep into the mound. When the height of the second course stones was known (51 inches) an additional portion of the mound was leveled off in the same manner and the second layer of core stones and pre-milled casing stones were placed to form the second layer; the perimeter faces of both courses were made flush with each other.

This process of laying, leveling and aligning the perimeter casing stones and core blocks (and then infill stones) continued up to the top of the seventh course of stones at about 26 feet, 7 inches above the base, which is roughly level with the top of the original mound and the proposed height of the Enclosure Wall.

Concurrent with the clearing of excess rock over the 13-acre pyramid footprint, work was underway on the construction of an adjacent harbor that occupied the natural terrain afforded by the Central Wadi (Image 3.1, middle left). This was a natural gulley created by runoff of the then frequent rains (and less frequent flashfloods) from the Giza Plateau. The current topography still indicates that under the high inundation levels of the Nile, the wadi would have become filled with the river's excess flow and had only to be improved during the previous dry season to retain the floodwater and allow its use as a harbor for construction purposes.

Other Site Work

An army of carpenters was also at work constructing numerous wooden sledges by which the individual stones were moved. Boats, barges, floats and sledges were being constructed of available timbers, some of the highly prized cedar requisitioned from the Mediterranean forests of Byblos[1] (Lebanon) to transport the stockpiled stone. Wooden tracks were being laid as skid ways to facilitate the movement of the stones from quarry down to dock at the shoreline. The stones on their sleds then were moved from dock to barge and from barge to the jobsite. Wooden components for a variety of uses were also being fabricated for incorporation in elements ranging from weirs to gates and from temporary housing to tools and furniture.

Masons and bricklayers were also hard at work to complete temporary housing for the workmen's encampment and to provide shelter for the proverbial "butcher, baker and candlestick maker" activities required to provide for the daily material needs of the personnel. Metallurgists needed foundries for tool making and for the maintenance of chisels and other tools.

All this activity required a squadron of scribes, our modern-day "clerks of the works", under the direction of the Vizier to keep track of orders, deliveries, schedules and payments, to ensure an organized jobsite and to monitor daily progress. Completion of all these concurrent site preparation activities allowed the Egyptians to then proceed with construction of the monument proper.

1.   Gilbert, Gregory "Ancient Egyptian Sea Power" Chapter 9, page 85

Chapter 4 – Lower Pyramid Elements

The following material presents how we envision water being used as the motive force in construction of the Great Pyramid.

The presence of the Nile River afforded the Ancient Egyptians that most sought after desert commodity, fresh water, and in abundant quantities. Water was also available to the Egyptians in the form of desert oases. Oases, as their name implies, are sources of life-giving waters found in otherwise hostile desert environments. This water appeared at the surface through fractures in the underlying limestone strata that released the water from confined aquifers below.

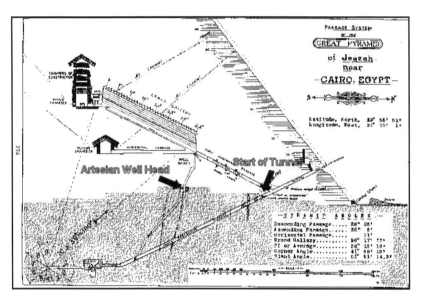

Image 4.1 – Cross section of Great Pyramid. (Authors added arrows and labels)
Source: Smyth, Charles Piazzi, <u>Life and Work at the Great Pyramid</u>. London: Wm. Isbister Ltd.
1880

Image 4.1 is from one of the earliest books on the Great Pyramid and is intriguing to us for several reasons. First, the lower shaded portion of the image shows an awareness that the native rock base under the pyramid was not level and had terraces or steps carved in it to form a foundation for the first layers of pyramid stones. Second, it shows the highest point of the native rock is where the Well and the Grotto are located. Third, the fissures in the native rock are also shown, with one fissure located adjacent to the well.

41

Well and Grotto

We believe the Grotto area was the location of a flowing artesian well that had been in existence long before the pyramid was built. It may be that the Grotto was an early improvement to the naturally occurring well located at the top of the limestone outcrop; it could have been a potable water supply accessible to the local community.

Image 4.2 shows a cross section of the Well Shaft and Grotto fitted with ten courses of limestone blocks on the sidewalls. There are footholds and handholds in different places along the extent of the vertical shaft to allow man-access from the top to the bottom. In spite of its name (given by the experts), the Well Shaft has never been actually considered (by the experts) to be a well, but as an escape route for workers leaving the *King's Chamber** after internment to avoid being trapped by the portcullis stones lowered into the *Ascending Corridor**, which were placed to prevent entry into the presumed tomb.

A red granite block at the edge of the deep hole in the Grotto has a hole drilled in it and its function is a mystery. Other red granite plugs located within the pyramid have been used to block corridors and this one could have been used to control water flow at some time.

*Phase 2 Pyramid Elements

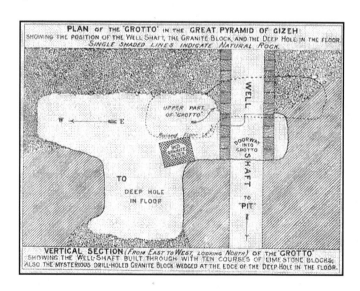

Image 4.2 - E-W Cross Section of Grotto and Well Shaft
Source: J & M Edgar

Descending Corridor

In Chapter 2, we indicated that it is our belief that the tunnel (Descending Corridor) at the Great Pyramid was excavated to reach the underlying permeable rock strata that contained artesian water under pressure. Perhaps the natural water flow from the existing artesian well fluctuated with the seasons, or from year to year, and a more reliable source was required throughout the construction period, which was going to be many years. The Ancient Egyptians had the expertise to drill through rock and mine tunnels so they planned a long shallow tunnel to reach a more powerful aquifer that they knew was below the well. A sloping tunnel is much easier to dig than a vertical well shaft, so they started the Descending Corridor right at the surface of the natural rock at a distance and angle designed to by-pass the existing well improvements and extend to the primary aquifer below. The line that exists between the live rock of the desert floor and the masonry construction above can be seen within the Descending Corridor today.

There was an interval of time to work on the Descending Corridor before the primary aquifer was reached because the natural well was providing enough water to selectively flood and level the site, probably using temporary mud brick retaining walls; excess water could drain back, following its natural path, down the slope of the Giza plateau to the River Nile.

Image 4.1 shows the Descending Corridor continuing upward above the level of the original well font where it ends at the Entrance Door on the north face of the pyramid. Allegedly, this opening was originally sealed by a hinged entry door not visible from the outside *(see Upper Pyramid Elements, Chapter 8)*.

The outside entrance to the Descending Corridor is located at the 13th stone course of the pyramid core blocks, extending down through the built construction into the live rock of the Giza Plateau, a total length of approximately 345 feet. At the bottom, a Horizontal Corridor continues southerly approximately 29 feet, ultimately connecting to the Subterranean Chamber, located approximately 100 feet below the level of the Enclosure Wall courtyard.

When Caviglia cleared the Descending Corridor of over 200 feet of rubble (1816-1819), a short distance of about 25 feet up from the Horizontal Corridor leading to the Subterranean Chamber, he found an opening in the Descending Corridor west sidewall that revealed a vertical shaft-way found to connect through the Well and Grotto area to the *Ascending Corridor** at the bottom of the *Grand Gallery**.   The vertical shaft-way has been presumed to be the escape route for workers sealing the *King's Chamber** from unauthorized entry after internment; it has also been theorized that it allowed entry into the chamber after the Pharaoh's internment for inspection and maintenance purposes.   Other than the Ascending Corridor, no further openings into or from the Descending Corridor have been found.

*Upper Pyramid Elements (Chapter 8)

The Subterranean Chamber

The Subterranean Chamber (Image 4.3) resides below the Giza Plateau some 100-feet and is accessed by the Descending Corridor; it is the first such chamber in pyramid history ever to have been hewn out of solid bedrock.   It consists of a large room approximately 13.8 x 8.1 x 3.3 meters high (46 x 27 x 11 feet high), with a dead-end corridor that extends off the west side some 53 feet.

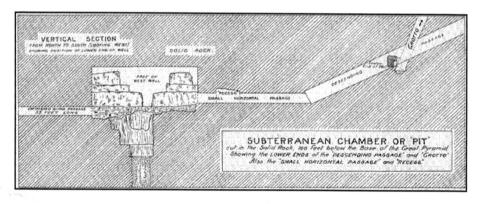

Image 4.3 Subterranean Chamber or "Pit"
Source: J & M Edgar

In the center of the room, but contiguous to the east wall, there is a vertical square-cut shaft (see Image 4.4) in the floor that extends down about 15 feet before rubble and debris is encountered; apparently this shaft extends to a depth of 60 feet when cleared.

The purpose of the Subterranean Chamber was previously unknown; there are no granite stones blocking the entrance. The floor is cut in several rough levels and unfinished.

The walls and floor of the chamber appear to have been worn or eroded (see Image 4.5), while the ceiling has been finished smooth and flat. There is a small unfinished niche in the Horizontal Corridor leading to the chamber. The Descending Corridor is too narrow to have accommodated a stone sarcophagus, so it is not considered to have ever been the destination of the Pharaoh's remains.[1]

Image 4.4 - View of the Square-Cut Well Shaft in the Subterranean Chamber.
Source: http://www.touregypt.net/featurestories/greatpyramid3.htm   1/31/2010

Image 4.5 - Internal View of the Subterranean Chamber.
The floor and walls appear to be eroded, while the ceiling is flat and smooth.
Source: http://gizapyramid.com/newtour6.htm   4/30/2010

The eroded condition of the inside of this chamber supports our theory that water gushing from the aquifer passed through this chamber for an extended period.

1. Material for this chapter was taken from Tour Egypt, The Pyramid of Khufu at Giza in Egypt, The Pyramid Proper, Part II: Internal and Substructure, by Alan Winston. http://gizapyramid.com/newtour6.htm 4/30/2010

Chapter 5 – Causeway Delivery System

A "Causeway" is defined as an elevated roadway. However, we believe that Khufu's Causeway was actually a series of water locks and that the Great Pyramid was built by transporting the huge stones directly from the Nile to the pyramid construction site on floating barges through a series of water locks, filled by the flow of artesian water naturally available at that location.

The remains of Khufu's Causeway no longer exist and modern day experts believe that the Pharaoh's funerary procession marched up the Causeway to the pyramid after his death. Those same experts do not see the Causeway as having been involved in the delivery of stones but seem to support the theory that the Ancient Egyptians delivered most of the stones from the quarry southwest of the pyramid, by virtue of a mega-ramp.

Many configurations of ramps have been conceived of, but the straight-on approach to the south face of the pyramid seems to be the most favored by Egyptologists. Such a mega-ramp extending to the top of the pyramid would reach perhaps a mile and one-half in length, assuming a slope between 5° to 7°, alleged by the experts to be flat enough to drag stones up to the working platform, with a team of workers pulling on ropes. A ramp of this magnitude would approach as much as five times the volume of the pyramid itself!

The Khufu pyramid was built on a plateau at an elevation of 60 meters AMSL and its Causeway descended to a level about 25 meters AMSL, then it is assumed that it made a slight bend to the north and continued to below the 20 meter elevation (the exact configuration is unknown). The other two Giza pyramids have their Valley Temples located at approximately 25 meters AMSL. Since they were built later than Khufu's pyramid we must assume that the Nile levels were adequate during those construction periods.

It may have been an unusually low Nile level coinciding with the building of Khufu's pyramid that inspired the Egyptians to attempt to construct the Sadd-Al-Kafara Dam referred to in Chapter 2, perhaps to create a construction holding pond for the Great Pyramid up river, by damming the river at Wadi Al-Garawi. When this failed it may be that they decided to extend the Causeway to the unusually low Nile level.

The Enclosure Wall, the Descending Corridor and the Subterranean Chamber together with the Mortuary Temple, the Causeway, and the Valley Temple were begun concurrently with the leveling of the site and were required to be finished together so that they could work in unison to facilitate the remaining construction requirements. Herodotus, in his "Histories", circa 450 BCE, stated that the Causeway took ten years to build and was finished first (before the pyramid).

> "*It took ten years' oppression of the people to make the causeway[2] **for the conveyance of the stones** (emphasis by the Authors), a work not much inferior, in my judgment, to the pyramid itself. This causeway is five furlongs (5/8 mile) in length, ten fathoms (60 ft) wide, and in height at the highest part, eight fathoms (48 ft). It is built of polished stone and is covered with carvings of animals. It took ten years, as I said – or rather to make the causeway, the works on the mound[3] where the pyramid stands, and the underground chambers ...*"

> [2] *The remains of two causeways still exist – the northern one, which is the largest, corresponding with the great pyramid, as the other does with the third.*

> [3] *This was leveling the top of the hill to form a platform. A piece of rock was also left in the center as a nucleus on which the pyramid was built.* [1]

Valley Temple

Egyptologists hold that the Valley Temple was located at the shores of the lowest level of the River Nile and was used for ritual purposes. We believe that the "Valley Temple", in its formative stages, was simply the first in a series of water locks that allowed the stones to be off-loaded from large delivery barges to smaller barges that conveyed the stones up the Causeway lock system to the "Mortuary Temple" or upper lock and through the Enclosure Wall into the Enclosure Pond.

In the 1980s, while sewerage work was underway in the streets of the village of Nazlet-es-Samman, basalt paving stones, presumed to be a portion of ruins of some ancient construction, were apparently found northeast of the pyramid, just beyond the edge of the desert. Dr. Zahi Hawass announced a connection between the basalt pavement and Khufu's Valley Temple; unfortunately, the Temple and Causeway connection have never been completely examined or verified.

At about 300 meters from the Valley Temple, the Causeway turned more westerly and continued on to the Mortuary Temple, located adjacent to the Great Pyramid's east face. Its total length as estimated by Dr. Hawass was

825 meters, although Herodotus wrote it was more on the order of 1,000 meters in length.

The Egyptologist Dr. Mark Lehner has stated that he believes the supporting structure of the causeway once rose to about 40 meters (132 feet) in height. He may have based his projection on the physical reality of having to extend a "corridor" *(sic)* flush, or level with the edge of the plateau, out to the estimated location of the Valley Temple. Presumably, a level walkway would have facilitated the royal funerary procession in its trek to the Pharaoh's resting place.

We also believe that construction of both the Valley and Mortuary Temples was completed per the final design as ritual temples only after completion of the construction of the monument.

Causeway and Locks

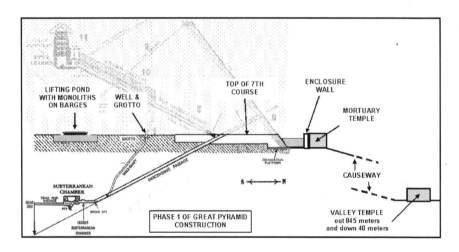

Image 5.1 Phase 1 pyramid elements north-south cross section.
Causeway and locks shown for illustration are actually located on the east façade.
Source: The Authors

In this section, we will explain how the Causeway locks conveyed the huge stones from the River Nile to the pyramid construction site. Our theory postulates that the Subterranean Chamber, Well and Grotto, Descending Corridor, Font Pond, Enclosure Wall, Mortuary Temple, Causeway, and Valley Temple were all components in Phase-1 of the stone delivery system (see Image 5.1) that gave continuity throughout the year to the transportation waterway path from the Nile up to the working level of the pyramid construction site.

The Enclosure Wall, built to a height of approximately 8 meters (26 feet, Dr. Lehner), surrounded the pyramid and created a 10 meter (33 feet) wide Courtyard and joined with the Mortuary Temple, which we propose acted as the uppermost lock in a series of locks that allowed the barges to come up the Causeway from the Nile.

Images 5.2 through 5.6 were produced by the authors using measurements taken from the Giza Plateau Mapping Project (see Bibliography). For clarity, the scales of the images vary to allow them to be represented with improved visual proportion within the text.

Image 5.2 shows the cross section of the plateau *along the path of the Causeway*. The total elevation drop along the path is from 60 meters AMSL to 20 meters AMSL, a total of 40 meters. From our perspective that means there must have been several locks to raise barges that height and distance. There is only a 5 meter drop out to 240 meters from the base of the pyramid. Then there is another drop of 30 meters at about 390 meters, then only another 5 meters of drop to the Valley Temple Lock.

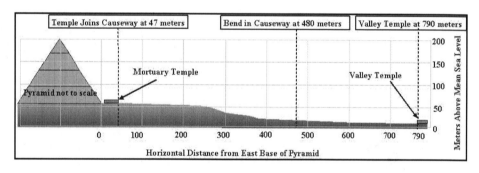

Image 5.2 Elevations along Causeway at the Great Pyramid. Source: The Authors

This indicates that most of the vertical drop of the lock system would have had to exist from the 240 meter point to the bend in the causeway at 480 meters; this represents a total drop of about 28 meters. This could be accomplished with three locks as shown in Image 5.5 below. It should be realized that parts of this lock system could have been underwater part of the year, and the lower portion (below the bend in the Causeway) could have been underwater all year, along with the Valley Temple lock, during years of high Nile inundation.

Image 5.3 shows the first seven courses of the pyramid and the Enclosure Pond filled up to the 6th course level. Adjacent is the Mortuary Temple lock filled to the same height with a barge loaded with stones waiting to enter the Enclosure Pond.

Image 5.4 shows Lock #2, which at 193 meters, is the longest and shallowest of all the upper locks and is the one used most throughout the year. The Nile at full flood would feed directly into this lock.

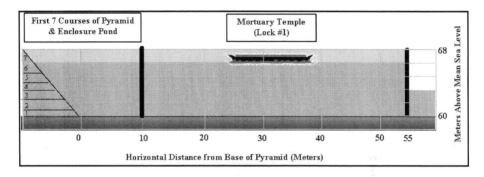

Image 5.3 Pyramid Lock #1 in the Causeway Lock System - Source: The Authors

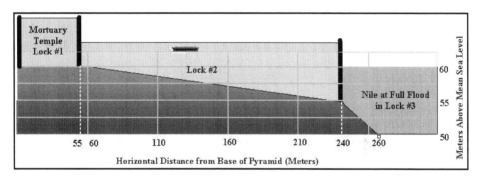

Image 5.4 - Lock #2 in the Causeway Lock System - Source: The Authors

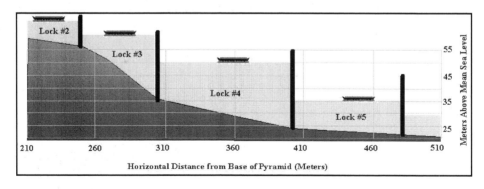

Image 5.5 - Locks #3, #4, and #5 in the Causeway Lock System - Source: The Authors

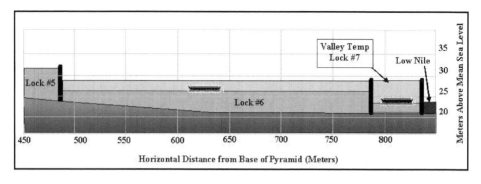

Image 5.6 - Lock #6 and the Valley Lock in the Causeway Lock System. Source: The Authors

Image 5.5 shows the three main lifting locks spanning from the 240 meter point out to the 480 meter point, which is the bend in the Causeway. These three locks are responsible for lifting barges from 22 to 55 meters or a total of 33 meters in height.

Image 5.6 shows Lock #6 and the Valley Temple lock, which together are the longest and most shallow of all the locks and are responsible for serving the delivery system during the lowest Nile levels. These could be underwater part of the year.

These seven locks are responsible for floating all the stones up to the pyramid construction site. It is likely that the Causeway locks themselves were built from the pyramid down towards the Nile with the large foundation stones delivered by barges during the inundation. Later, the locks would also supply stones for Phase 2 of the delivery system, which raised the individual stones up the pyramid above the seventh course.

To reiterate, Herodotus indicated the completed Causeway was 10 fathoms (60 feet) wide and 8 fathoms (48 feet) high at the highest point.

As a comparison, the Willamette Locks in the state of Oregon, USA http://www.willamettefalls.org/HisLocks) have seven gates in four chambers which lift up to 15.5 meters (50 feet) elevation change (depending on tides and river flow) with a usable width of 11.2 meters (37 feet), very similar to Herodotus' statement.

Mortuary Temple

Image 5.7 shows the reconstructed plan of Khufu's Mortuary Temple. The uppermost black line represents the pyramid's east wall and below it the parallel black line is the Enclosure Wall with the limestone pavement of the Courtyard between them. Below that is the square outline of the Mortuary Temple that is contiguous with the Enclosure Wall, illustrating the complex layout with many pillars and a basalt paved floor area. Below that is the start of the Causeway heading off slightly north of east; adjacent are several boat pits and the smaller Queen's Pyramid.

We suggest that many of the features of this Causeway lock system were later transformed from mere foundation and site development structures into more formal uses such as the Mortuary and Valley temples when their construction functions were completed.

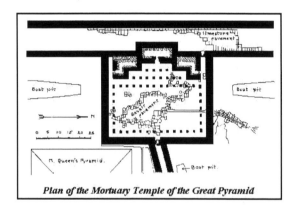

Plan of the Mortuary Temple of the Great Pyramid

Image 5.7 Reconstructed Plan of the Mortuary Temple at Khufu's Pyramid
Source: http://www.guardians.net/egypt/pyramids/GreatPyramid.htm   09/06/2009

Enclosure Wall

Egyptologists have historically placed symbolic and religious significance to most elements in the typical pyramid complex.   They believe that the Enclosure Wall provided security for the monument, keeping out all but those specifically authorized entry into the sanctuary. We believe that, at least initially, the Enclosure Wall actually functioned as a retaining wall for the supply water that powered the Causeway lock system.

According to an early estimate by Dr. Mark Lehner, the Enclosure Wall was approximately 8 meters in height (26 feet) and was located approximately 10 meters (33 feet) from the pyramid. The Enclosure Wall was connected to the Mortuary Temple, which was also connected to the Causeway. Presumably, after the Pharaoh's funerary procession reached the Mortuary Temple, various rituals were carried out before the procession continued into the Courtyard behind the Enclosure Wall. Recently, Dr. Lehner has re-estimated the height of this wall to approximately 10 feet, based on a subsequent evaluation of some of the remaining foundation stones. No other gates or entrances through the Enclosure Wall, other than at the Mortuary Temple, have ever been reported.

If the Enclosure Wall was indeed 26 feet high and acted as a retaining wall for water, it must have been thicker at the base than at the top. A typical retaining wall is always thicker at the base since the forces that it must resist are much higher at the bottom of the wall due to the pressure of the water behind it. Also, the wall was probably keyed or let into the bedrock to prevent it from slipping sideways by lateral displacement. Friction between the limestone layers may have provided the needed lateral stability for each course, but the courses may have also been keyed one to the other. We have seen renderings of typical Enclosure Walls illustrating this type of profile, similar to the one shown in Dr. Lehner's, *The Complete Pyramids*, page 19, where the standard pyramid complex is shown based on the pyramid of Unas. However, we have seen no dimensional data of the width of the base of the Enclosure Wall at the Great Pyramid.

Other Causeway Systems

What evidence is there for the Causeway to have been used as a lock system when so little remains to be examined? There are more complete remains of other Temple and Causeway systems, notably the adjacent Pyramid of Khafre and the Unas pyramid, adjacent to the Saqqara Pyramid complex have "Causeways" that are better preserved and look more like the channels (locks) that we claim they were built to be (see Image 5.10).

Image 5.8 shows the overall layout of Khafre's pyramid complex showing the nearby Sphinx and its temple location. This Causeway is 494.6 meters long in contrast with the estimated length of Khufu's causeway at 825 meters (Dr. Hawass). The image also shows the stone perimeter wall around the pyramid, which is said to have enclosed a space or courtyard 10 meters wide paved with limestone slabs of irregular form.

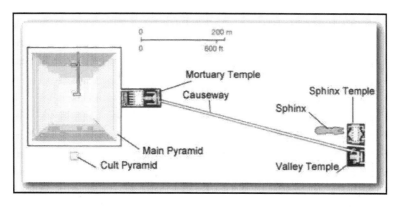

Image 5.8 Khafre's Temple/Causeway System
Source: http://touregypt.net/featurestories/khafrep.htm   9/06/2009

Image 5.9 shows schematic views of Khafre's Mortuary and Valley Temples. It is quite likely, as we mentioned before, that they were designed with a dual purpose. The initial use as a water lock was obsolete after the pyramid building process was complete and the superstructure was reused and redecorated as a temple. This is not so strange an assumption because the locks acted as portals for the stone-laden barges to pass through during construction and later, when converted to temples, were the portals through which the Pharaoh was expected to pass on his journey to eternity.

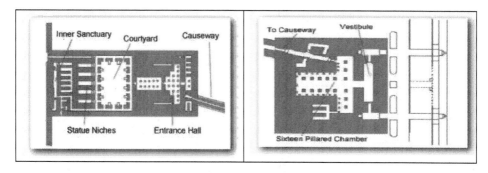

Image 5.9 Close up schematic views of Khafre's Mortuary and Valley Temples
Source: http://touregypt.net/featurestories/khafrep.htm   09/06/2009

The following is a passage from the above source (see Image 5.9) describing the valley temple above right.

> "The causeways connected the Nile canal with two separate entrances on the Valley temple facade that were sealed **by huge, single-leaf doors** (emphasis by the Authors) probably made of cedar wood and hung on copper hinges. Each of these doorways was

protected by a recumbent Sphinx. The northern most of these portals was dedicated to the goddess Bastet, while the southern portal was dedicated to Hathor..."

The mention of huge single leaf doors is reminiscent of the huge wooden doors which exist in modern day operating locks on large rivers and canals. The authors live quite close to the Willamette Locks in West Linn, Oregon, which were opened in 1873. There are seven gates in four chambers which lift up to 50 feet (15.5 meters) elevation change (depending on river flow) with a usable width of 37 feet (11.2 meters). The system is 3,565 feet long (1,087 meters), which is longer than the Khufu Causeway. It can accommodate vessels up to 175 feet (53.3 meters) long. Each of the four concrete constructed chambers is 210 feet by 40 feet. As originally built, the massive lock gates and the water transfer valves were manually operated. In the 1940's electrically driven hydraulic systems replaced manual operation. It originally took fourteen workers to manually operate the locks, but today it takes just two.

Image 5.10 shows the remains of Khafre's Causeway on the left and the Unas Causeway on the right. Both resemble channels or aqueducts more than they indicate roadways or viaducts and support our theory that the Causeways were essentially waterways with locks for the transport of stones on barges. They were built to the dimensions that would allow loaded barges to travel back and forth along the Causeway between the Mortuary Temple and the Valley Temple. The first stones would have been the largest and determined the necessary dimensions for the Causeway.

Image 5.10 Remains of Khafre's pyramid causeway (left) and the Unas causeway (right).
Source: http://egyptphoto.ncf.ca/pyramid%20of%20Khafre%20causeway.htm 09/06/2009

As a further indication of the use of water on the Giza Plateau, the following quote describes dock-like remains between the Mortuary and Valley Temples of the Khafre pyramid.

> *"The broad terrace to the east of Khafre's pyramid is made of massive limestone blocks weighing up to hundreds of tons. Huge limestone piers project beyond the northeast and southwest (sic) corners of the terrace,* **looking like slipways or giant docks** *(emphasis by the Authors). Five narrow boat-shaped trenches carved into the natural rock extend into the recesses between the two piers and the mortuary temple."*[2]

1. George Rawlinson, *Herodotus, The Histories*, Book II, Chapter 124.
2. Mark Lehner, *The Complete Pyramids*, p. 123.

Chapter 6 – First Seven Courses

We consider it significant that the first seven course thicknesses of the pyramid together total 319 inches or 26 feet 7 inches (according to Lemesurier, see Chart, Appendix A.15). This corresponds to Dr. Mark Lehner's original estimate of the height of the Enclosure Wall at about 26 feet, which was apparently based on the width of the remnants of the footings found on site. As we previously mentioned, this is also the approximate height of the original artesian well opening improved at the surface of the bedrock at the top of the Giza outcrop.

We hold that the relationship between these three elements is not a coincidence. The Well/Grotto represents an ancient improvement of a naturally-occurring artesian well; there was probably water flowing out of the artesian well at the well head during ancient times.

The ancient builders must have known they could build a wall around the pyramid to retain the water to fill the Enclosure Pond to deliver stones to the height of the Well/Grotto. They also may have known that the artesian water, when confined, might flow to an even greater height than the Well/Grotto, but did not necessarily know how high. The potentiometric height of a flowing artesian well, although measurable by trial and error, may not have been well understood in ancient times.

Enclosure Wall Construction

It is likely that the first course of stones of the Enclosure Wall were laid in the same way and at the same time as the first course of the pyramid. A mud brick retaining wall could have been formed around the pyramid site high enough (say 1-2 meters) for the barges containing the first course of stones (including the cornerstones, casing stones and major monoliths) to be floated in, with the first courses of the Enclosure Wall built just inside the mud brick wall. This would have afforded enough freeboard for the delivery vessels.

After the first couple of courses of pyramid stones and Enclosure Wall stones were in place the mud brick wall would have been removed. As stated in Chapter 5, it makes sense that the first layer of stones in the Enclosure Wall may have been keyed into the bedrock footing to give the wall more stability. Likewise each successive course of stone in the wall could have been keyed into the one below it to maintain wall stability up to a height of 26 feet; the structural integrity of the Enclosure Wall under pressure from the weight of water in the Enclosure Pond, had a finite limit. However, in fact, the friction offered by the rough stone surfaces may have been sufficient to resist the lateral water pressure forces.

Enclosure Pond

As previously mentioned, in order for barges coming up the Causeway lock system to deliver the first course of stones into the Enclosure Pond, there would have to have been sufficient depth of water to float the barges. The draft of a typical barge could have been several feet and the vessel also would have had a freeboard height of several feet[1]. The stones comprising the first course or two probably were slid off the barge on their sledges directly onto the working platform surface of the course immediately below the one under construction. It is probable that special barges, smaller than the Nile barges, were built for use in the Causeway locks and Enclosure Pond so that they could be maneuvered in the more confined space.

After having delivered the initial stones from the Valley Temple lock, up the Causeway to construct the first course, the water level inside the Enclosure Wall was adjusted up to a level that flushed the top of the working platform with that of the freeboard of the barge. Then the stones could be directly off–loaded to the working platform. This required that the outer lock gate at the top of the Causeway be closed to allow the water level in the Mortuary Temple lock to increase to the appropriate height.

After the water levels on both sides of the gate were equal, a loaded barge in the lock could be transferred through the inner gate into the Enclosure Pond. In this manner, stones were off-loaded directly onto their level as previously indicated, onto the pyramid platform where they were quickly ushered to their pre-determined permanent location and incorporated into the pyramid construction.

Concurrently, an empty barge could enter the Mortuary Temple lock, the water level dropped to match the level in Lock #2 (see Image 5.4) and the barge could make its way back down to the Nile. At the same time, work was underway completing the extension of the Causeway and its lock system downward towards the lower level of the Nile; Lock #2 would be serviceable during the inundation without the lower locks being utilized.

Font Pond

At the same time as the laying of the first courses of stones, a special pond or "Font Pond," was being readied inside the pyramid footprint to accommodate barges that were carrying the large monoliths for later incorporation in the upper levels of the pyramid. These special barges were moored within the Font Pond and sequestered there as the construction level rose around them.

The Font Pond itself was raised at the completion of each successive course of construction *through the principle of displacement.* The bottom of the pond was in-filled with core stones to maintain a suitable depth so that the pond was raised with the construction, level by level. The Font Pond was also able to move laterally with each successive layer, a feature that later allowed its location to be superimposed over the top of the Well Shaft/Grotto.

When the inundation level was high, the lower portion of the Causeway was short-circuited with the stone-laden barges being guided into the Causeway at the point where the high water level impinged upon the Causeway; the immersed portion was by-passed. The barges could then be directed into the Enclosure Pond through the Mortuary Temple lock at the junction of the Enclosure Wall and the Causeway. When the inundation receded, the route was lengthened as the Nile shoreline got lower and the barges had to come up a lengthening Causeway with multiple locks.

First Seven Courses

The first seven stone courses of the Great Pyramid together represent about 16% of the total volume of the pyramid (see Appendix A.7). In our proposed method of construction, the stones were laid down one course at a time. Stones were delivered on barges floated up the Causeway lock system, through the Mortuary Temple lock and into the Enclosure Pond behind the Enclosure Wall. The water level was elevated for each course under construction by controlling the outflow of the water through the lock gates at the Mortuary Temple lock.

Image 6.1 illustrates courses 4 through 7 showing a barge floating in the Enclosure Pond and offloading a stone to the seventh course. The Enclosure Wall height around the Enclosure Pond is shown at the same level as the top of the seventh course and is at approximately the same level as the top of the natural artesian well. The 52 degree angle shown in Image 6.1 is the face angle of the pyramid.

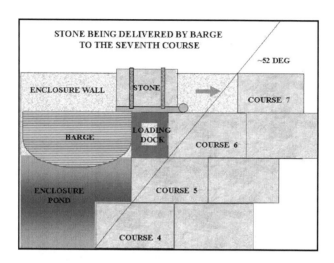

Image 6.1 Barge delivering a stone to the seventh course. Source: The Authors

The barge in the image above is shown at the highest level at which it could unload stones directly onto the pyramid, since this height coincides with the maximum height of the Enclosure Wall as determined by the aforementioned site conditions and the experience of the Ancient Egyptians.

Any higher than this and the water would overflow the Enclosure Wall. Consequently, another method of raising stones above the seventh course had to be found in order to complete the upper levels of construction. Details of this subsequent method are described in Phase 2 Construction, which follows in Chapter 8.

1. Gilbert, Gregory, *Ancient Egyptian Sea Power*, Chapter 9, page 85.

Chapter 7 – Phase 1 Water Flow

We discussed in detail in Chapter 1 how the unique features of the River Nile and its geology provided the Egyptians with the necessary raw materials and the means of transport by which to deliver them. We have discussed the presence of artesian water and the manner in which the Ancient Egyptians were exposed to this knowledge. Also discussed was the likelihood of their hydrologists and well diggers combining their expertise to harness the power inherent in the aquifer. We have also described Phase 1 of a stone delivery system that provided the means to float barge loads of stones up the Causeway locks and into the Enclosure Pond, behind the Enclosure Wall to complete the first seven courses of the pyramid. In order for the water locks to function, a water source had to be continuously available to the system, *at a level higher*, than the highest level of construction. This will be discussed in detail in the following section.

Volume of Water Required

Our theory proposes that the Great Pyramid was built using the displacement power of water. We have calculated (see Appendix, A.12) how much water would be required to lift (or float) all the stones in the Great Pyramid. We determined the pyramid's volume to be just over 2.6 million cubic meters (92 million cubic feet). In order to calculate how much water was needed to float the stones, we conducted the following calculation.

Since stone is approximately two and one half times the density of water, the volume of water required to displace this amount of stone would be approximately two and one half times the volume of stone. This results in just over 6.5 million cubic meters (230 million cubic feet) of water.

According to historical assertions, the Great Pyramid was built in approximately twenty years; therefore, utilizing this time frame, we can determine what delivery rate of water was required. This is shown in Appendix A.12 to be 22 cubic feet per minute or 164 US gallons per minute; a surprisingly small flow rate when considering the size of the monument. A very small flowing artesian well can produce this amount of water, which represents a pipe three to four inches in diameter (see Appendix A.13). A few instances of similarly sized copper pipes have been found around the Fourth Dynasty pyramids (see Appendix A.27).

As mentioned previously, the first seven courses of the pyramid accounted for only about 16% of the total stones (not accounting for the keystone of live rock incorporated into the monument) so 84% of the bulk of the pyramid was left to be constructed above the seventh course. This portion of the construction process is described in Phase 2 Construction, beginning with Chapter 8.

Artesian Well Flow Rates

Lacking the historical water flow rates of the Giza artesian well, we sought information on general artesian well flow rates (see Appendix A.14). Information indicates estimated flow rates from 128 artesian wells in a water management district in Florida, USA and illustrates an average flow rate of 25.5 cubic feet per minute...very close to our required flow rate of 22 cubic feet per minute from the Giza artesian well, derived in Appendix A.12.

Water Course

Before the pyramid was built, the natural artesian well was overflowing in the Grotto area and probably flowing down the Giza plateau in a southeasterly direction following the topography down to the River Nile. At this early time it was probably used as a community water source. When the pyramid was started, this flow of water was redirected to assist with the flooding required to level the site. Then, as the pyramid foundation was begun, the flow was used to fill various site leveling ponds that eventually were retired. Then the flow filled the Font Pond within the pyramid footprint where the monoliths on their barges were floated and was finally redirected to the permanent Enclosure Pond.

We have estimated the Enclosure Pond volume to be over 98,000 cubic meters (3.5 million cubic feet) in Appendix A.17. At our minimum required flow rate of 22 cubic feet per minute, the Enclosure Pond would take 109 days to fill to the top, but only a fraction of that time to be able to float the first barges delivering the stones for the first few courses. We have estimated the volume of Lock #1 (Mortuary Temple) at over 7,200 cubic meters in Appendix A.18. This lock could be filled using only 1/8 of the water in a full Enclosure Pond. So the Enclosure Pond is an adequate reservoir for operating a Causeway lock system. It was continually replenished from the artesian well, especially so during "off-peak" periods such as the hours of darkness when the locks were likely not in operation.

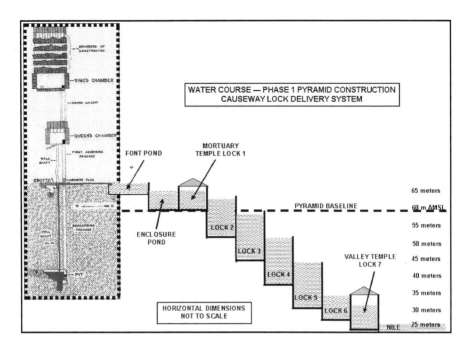

Image 7.1 Schematic of water course from Subterranean Pit through locks to Nile – Source: Authors

Image 7.1 superimposes one of the original Piazzi Smyth drawings of the east-west cross section of the Great Pyramid over our schematic of the water flow in the locks. The water in the subterranean aquifer is shown in the "pit', then flowing up the Well Shaft to the Well and Grotto area where it fed into the Font Pond, which floats the monolith barges upwards within the pyramid footprint with each construction level. The Font Pond overflow fed into the Enclosure Pond and Mortuary Temple lock where the water level was controlled by gates to regulate the height of the water in the Enclosure Pond. Overflow water constantly drained down the lock system and additional water flowed with each lock operation. In this way the same displacement water was used several times during the overall lock cycle before it emerged at the bottom lock into the River Nile.

End of Phase 1 Construction

PHASE 2 CONSTRUCTION

Tefnut Goddess of Water

Upper Pyramid Elements

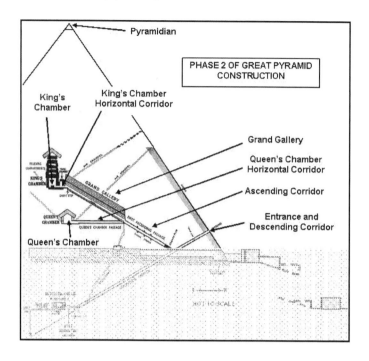

Image 8.0 - Upper pyramid elements. Source: The Authors
See Chapters 8 through 12

As with Phase 1 construction, a concise accounting and understanding of the construction process requires the reader have some knowledge of the physical features of the site and structure. The elements listed below had to be completed in chronological order to facilitate the pyramid construction above the seventh course of stones. Many of these activities were pursued concurrently, and each element is described in detail in Chapter 9. Since our theory's construction engine relies on the power of water, we will begin discussion of Phase 2 Construction in Chapter 8, with the "Water Stairs", the element that made construction above the seventh course possible.

Entrance and Descending Corridor	Original entrance to the pyramid
Ascending Corridor	Corridor to the Grand Gallery
Queen's Chamber Corridor	Corridor to the Queen's Chamber
Queen's Chamber	Chamber located at the centerline
Grand Gallery	Large corbelled inclined hallway
King's Chamber Corridor	Corridor to the King's Chamber
King's Chamber	Topmost chamber in the pyramid

Chapter 8 – Water Stairs

As mentioned, construction above the seventh course of stones was made possible by the "Water Stairs". The term is descriptive of the function of this element; namely, floating individual stones up a series of wooden lock boxes arranged in stair-step fashion. In this Chapter we will discuss how the individual stones were lifted to each subsequent level, all the way to the top of the construction platform wherever it was located and how each higher level was negotiated.

Herodotus

George Rawlinson (1812-1902) in his 1881 translation of Herodotus' "The Histories", Chapter 125, uses the following English words:

> *"The pyramid was built in steps[1], battlement-wise, as it is called, or, according to others, altar-wise. After laying the stones for the base, they raised the remaining stones to their places by means of* **machines formed of short wooden planks** *(emphasis by the Authors). The first machine raised them from the ground to the top of the first step. On this there was another machine, which received the stone upon its arrival, and conveyed it to the second step, whence a third machine advanced it still higher. Either they had as many machines as there were steps in the pyramid, or possibly they had but a single machine, which, being easily moved, was transferred from tier to tier as the stone rose – both accounts are given, and therefore I mention both.* **The upper portion of the pyramid was finished first, then the middle, and finally the part which was lowest and nearest the ground** *(emphasis by the Authors)."*

> *1. These steps, or successive stages, had their faces nearly perpendicular, or at an angle of about 75^0, and the triangular space, formed by each projecting considerably beyond the one immediately above it, was afterwards filled in, thus completing the general form of the pyramid. (See Image 8.3).*

Several translations of Herodotus' "Histories" have been completed throughout the years and the choice of words utilized by various translators to depict Herodotus' true meaning has led various scholars to different interpretations and therefore different paths in their quest to solve the construction methods employed in the Great Pyramid. For example, some translators have chosen the word "lever" where others have used "tool" or "machine". Obviously, all levers could be considered tools, and a compilation or assembly of levers could be considered a machine; *but certainly not all tools or machines are levers.* The distinction is an extremely important one, since a clear understanding of the term intended could have vastly different implications and thus greatly alter any conclusions drawn. Indeed, many sophisticated methods of construction of the Great Pyramid have been devised and proposed utilizing a system of levers, one of the more recent of which being Martin Isler's *"Sticks, Stones and Shadows"*, 2001. Nonetheless, the currently most favored method of transporting the blocks utilizes nothing more than a construction mega-ramp, whether straight, spiral, indented, external or internal or a combination. The method we describe here follows none of those.

Rawlinson's translation suggests that Herodotus intended to indicate that the method used by the Ancient Egyptians in transporting the blocks, employed the use of *"machines formed of short wooden planks"*. He also indicates that these machines were employed at each level of the pyramid, whether by dismantling and reconstructing the machine at each subsequent level, or by simply adding another machine.

It's worthwhile to note at this point, that Herodotus has been discredited, even vilified, for several of his writings, especially the passage that relates the Pharaoh's abuse of his daughter as chattel for raising construction funds. Truthful or not, it may be useful to remember that, although Herodotus recorded his observations and conducted his interviews some 2,000 years after the completion of the pyramid, his critics now offer their judgments of his writing some 2,500 years after it was penned!

Nonetheless, our proposed stone lifting system utilizes neither the lever nor ramp and avoids the extreme physical labor required to drag stones by rope up an inclined surface, including that of the face of the pyramid itself. Any stevedore, longshoreman or warehouseman will attest that there are two issues of primary importance associated with the transport of a heavy payload: 1) knowing in advance the destination and, 2) lifting it once, or as few times as possible. Any violation of these two premises results in an immediate doubling of the work effort required to achieve the desired result. In a project of the magnitude and scale of the Great Pyramid, any violation of these two principles would quickly outstrip the available funds, manpower, and schedule, resulting in its impending failure. It is precisely for this reason, and its associated implications, that we must reject any ramp or lever theory yet proposed.

In our scenario, the quarrymen were required to secure the quarried and finished blocks to a delivery vehicle; a wooden sled, or more properly, sledge.

The next time the block would be lifted from its sledge would be during its final placement, in its predetermined location in the pyramid, when it would be lifted manually for the second time and lowered from the sledge to the stone surface of the course below it. All intermediary movement of the block would be facilitated by sliding the sledge-mounted stone over prepared slipways, lubricated if required, comprised of wooden cleats set in the desert sands, or across wooden or stone docks, to the wooden decks of transport barges. The wooden barges would float up, down or across the Nile, up the Causeway lock system and into the Enclosure Pond.

Image 8.1 Cedar sledge from Lisht.
© Copyright Dieter Arnold, *Building in Egypt*, p. 276
Source: http://www.world-mysteries.com/mpl_2_1.htm 11/29/2009

Once the seventh course of pyramid construction had been completed (see Phase 1) and the water level in the Enclosure Pond had reached its maximum height, barges could not be raised further to supply stones above the seventh course, so another method of offloading the stones from their barges to the eighth course and above had to be designed and the Pharaoh's Vizier Hemiunu obliged. This is detailed in Phase 2 of our delivery system, a device or machine we term the "Water Stairs", which begins at the seventh course of the pyramid and continued up to the level under construction, until the topping out of the pyramid concluded with the placement of the capstone or Pyramidian.

Design

What is meant by the term "Water Stairs"? The Water Stairs are locks or lock boxes constructed of wooden timbers (*short wooden planks* of Lebanese Cedar), crafted by Egyptian master carpenters and lashed together with ropes and dowels, in the manner of their boats, and manned by the world's greatest hydrologists and seamen of their time, the Ancient Egyptians. The Water

Stairs were likely constructed at each course and were connected one to the other, to allow the conveyance of each sledge-mounted stone (or stones) to traverse from the bottom-most lock box, to the top-most lock box, wherever the upper working course was at the time. This continuous operation ran non-stop from sunup to sundown, hampered only by the lack of daylight, or a hiatus in the supply of blocks. Construction could have also taken place around the clock, during cloudless moonlit nights in the desert or even perhaps with the aid of flaming torches.

When each block had ascended to the current construction level, the top-most Water Stairs was opened, the stone-laden sledge was slid out, likely onto a pre-wetted gypsum pathway and the stone was quickly spirited to its pre-determined location. This is where the final lift occurred, when the stone was removed from its sledge, perhaps aided by the famed and enigmatic "wooden rocker", and lowered onto the top stone surface of the course immediately below. Other uses for this device have been suggested.

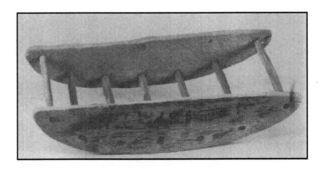

Image 8.2 The wooden rocker known at the "Petrie Rocker"
Source: http://www.haitheory.com   6/7/2010

But where were these Water Stairs situated? How were they secured to the pyramid face? How big were they? How did they work? And most importantly, where did the water required to operate the locks come from?

Fortunately for the Egyptians, the symbolic primordial earth-mound manifested as the pyramid is perfectly suited for this task. While the sloping faces of the Great Pyramid are inclined at approximately 52 degrees from the horizontal, two adjacent sloping faces converge at the corner creating a much shallower "arris" angle of approximately 42 degrees (see Appendix A.9). This shallower angle creates a larger footprint area at each level upon which to construct a series of wooden lockboxes, thereby affording a larger box with greater supporting area than would otherwise be available on the much smaller surface footprint area afforded by the face of the pyramid (see Image 8.3).

We postulate that, above the seventh course, the casing cornerstones were left uninstalled in order to leave a large triangular footprint on which to place the lockboxes or Water Stairs used to raise the stones up to the 8th course level and beyond (see Herodotus quote, above).

The Water Stairs were also literally tied one to the other as each level was completed and the subsequent higher box was then constructed to deliver the stones to the next level under construction. The result was not unlike a modern staircase, except that each individual tread (lockbox) was independently supported by the stone coursework immediately below it.

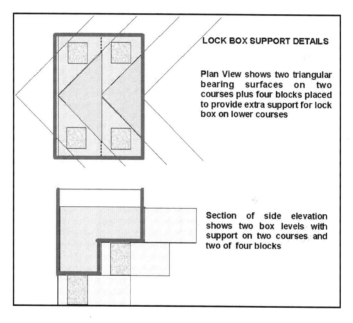

Image 8.3 Plan and elevation views of lockbox, or "Water Stairs", support. Source: The Authors

All four arris edges of the pyramid probably had Water Stairs constructed upon them. It is also probable that, at any one time, three of the Water Stairs were transporting stones upward to the working level, while the fourth was left to transport the empty wooden sledges back down to the Enclosure Pond. The sledges were comparatively light and small and could be stacked one upon the other, (like modern-day wood pallets) thereby freeing the other three corners to deliver the stones at the appropriate working platform at a maximum rate. The "recycling" of the sledges would continue in this manner until they were loaded onto barges, but this time, for their return trip to the quarries, where they would once again be loaded with an individual stone and the cycle would start anew.

The Water Stairs were sized big enough (approximately 8 feet deep by 10 feet wide) to transport the largest core block and casing stone utilized above the seventh course, together with its sledge, while accommodating enough room for each box's gates to open, thereby opening the passage for transport of the stone to the next higher course. When the self-contained floats housed within each Water Stairs were at equal levels, the sledge was slid off directly onto the next float, the doors were closed behind it, and the water level in the new Water Stairs was then increased, thereby raising the payload to the next level. The cycle was repeated over and over again until the last stone found its designated location within the monument.

The lifting of limestone blocks of this type and size dictates that the Water Stairs floats had to displace approximately two and one half times as much water volume as the volume of the stones (plus the weight of the wooden float and sledge). The thickest core block above the 7th course (other than possibly the Pyramidian) was located at course #35 and was approximately 127 cm (50 inches) thick.

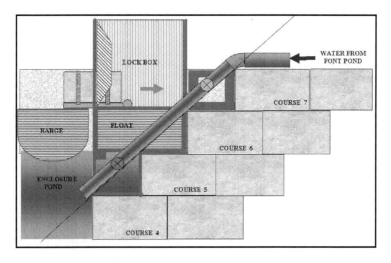

Image 8.4 The First Water Stair, or lock-box, in the Water Stairs. Source: The Authors

Image 8.4 is the Authors' rendering of one of the first four Water Stair lockboxes installed at each corner of the pyramid. It is a wooden lockbox founded on courses 4 and 5 and extending up to and above course #7. A wooden float, built in the same manner as Egyptian boats, fits inside the lock box; it displaces over two and one half times the volume of the largest stone and when it is at rest it is level with the freeboard of the barge so the stones on their sledges can be offloaded with ease to the same level. When the stone is loaded and the Water Stair gate(s) closed, water from a supply maintained in the Font Pond at the highest level of construction is directed through a valve from a supply pipe into the Water Stair. The water level rises and the float lifts the stone up to the eighth level at which time the valve is closed, the float comes to a hard stop-block at the higher level and the stone can be slid off over the wooden loading dock onto the eighth course.

We show how this translates into the required float volume of 4 cubic meters and lock box volume of about 8 cubic meters, in the Appendix A.15. Something of this size constructed of wood when viewed against the expansive backdrop of the pyramid would certainly look like a machine made of "short wooden planks", as Herodotus described.

Font Pond

The Font Pond was a water reservoir constructed at each working platform level beginning at the first course and fed by the water rising up from the artesian well head at the top of the seventh course. It maintained a head of water higher than the course under construction and its outflow was directed to the four corners of the working platform to feed the Water Stairs as required (see cover illustration). Surplus water filling the Font Pond simply by-passed the Water Stairs by means of the supply water line that allowed the water to return down alongside the Water Stairs back into the Enclosure Pond thereby eliminating surplus water in the work area. In addition to supplying water to the Water Stairs, the Font Pond was also being used to raise and maintain the flotilla of barges with their monoliths on board.

With this system in place, all the stones for the level under construction were delivered and placed before the Font Pond and its supply had to be raised up to the next level and four more Water Stairs were installed, one at each corner.

It seems likely that manpower to operate the Water Stairs may have required as many as three operators for each lock cycle; one for operating the valves and two for opening and closing the gates and moving the stone laden sledge. Obviously, workstations may have allowed one worker to do more than one job, thereby reducing the workforce required. It is also likely that the Water Stairs had wooden man-stairs attached, probably to both sides, to facilitate the workers transitioning from one Water Stairs to the other in the course of their work. In any event, this feature accounts for a massive reduction in the manpower requirement traditionally envisaged for the construction of the Great Pyramid.

Image 8.5 is a rendering of the elevated float enabling a stone to be slid off on to the eighth course and a second stone on the barge being made ready for transfer to the Water Stair in the next cycle after the float descends to its original position.

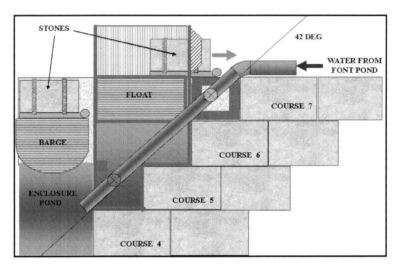

Image 8.5 Stone Delivered to the Eighth Course. Source: The Authors

Dynamics and Performance

We have dealt with the performance of the Water Stairs in detail in Appendix A.22. Initially we estimated the time it would take to displace a Water Stairs float of 4 cubic meters using a square wooden supply pipe of 8" x 8" (chosen to match the cross-sectional area of the Ventilation Shafts in the Queen's Chamber). That activity computed to just over 31 seconds. Then we estimated times for manual operations such as turning valves on and off and moving the stones from one float to another, and we obtained a lock box cycle time of approximately 3.5 minutes (see Appendix A.28).

In order to judge the performance of our Water Stairs against historical estimates of the time it took to build the pyramid, we made two calculations; one historical and the other using our 3.5 minute cycle time.

First, according to most historical accounts, it took approximately 20 years to place the estimated 2.3 million stones to build the pyramid. If this were true, then it would require the delivery of 315 stones per day. This is 26 stones per hour, assuming a 12-hour day.

Second, using three sets of Water Stairs to make the deliveries, and the estimated Water Stair exchange time of 3.5 minutes, one stone could be delivered every 1.17 minutes. This would amount to 70 stones per hour or 842 stones in a 12-hour day. This delivery rate computes to 2.3 million stones in about 7.5 years...much faster than the historical account and more in line with the 10 years remaining after Herodotus' estimate of the time taken to build the Causeway and its associated lower pyramid elements.

Since the Water Stairs only raise stones above the seventh course, they only had to lift 84% of the pyramid stones, or 1,932,000 stones. Using the same Water Stairs exchange rate of 3.5 minutes, this would take 6.3 years!

Another element that could improve the proposed delivery rate is the fact that the stones were smaller the further up the pyramid they were to be delivered. In Appendix A.6 we show that stone courses #7-106 averaged 34 inches thick, whereas stone courses #107-203 averaged 22 inches thick. With the smaller stones, the sledges and Water Stairs could deliver more than one stone at a time, thus reducing the required delivery time even further.

Chapter 9 - Pyramid Design

In this Chapter we will address a number of other well-documented details about the constructed elements of the pyramid, many of which we believe have been misinterpreted as to their purpose. As we shall see, quite a number of these elements are not only consistent with, but demanded by our theory of Floating Stones. Still, there are a number of significant elements of the construction which do not bear on our theory one way or the other, yet are too important to exclude. As a result, we will describe them here as well, indicating whether or not they are connected to our theory.

The elements identified in this Chapter had to be completed in relatively chronological order to facilitate the pyramid construction above the seventh course of stones. Many of these activities were pursued concurrently, and each element is described in detail below.

Design Characteristics

The question posed in the Introduction was "How is it then that the Great Pyramid has been able to withstand the ravages of time? What is it about its design and construction that has made it so durable?" What did the ancient Egyptians consider to be everlasting? The heavens and the movement of the heavenly bodies were important in their predictability. Immortality of the spirit was the foundation of their religion. The original mound of Earth's creation, the Ben Ben stone, or the original mound of Earth rising from the primordial abyss was also a fundamental creation concept of the Ancient Egyptians.

So a man-made pyramidal mountain of stone would seem like an obvious design for permanence. Before the Great Pyramid, at least one pyramid was constructed with steeper sides, and a few more with stones laid at a sloping angle. Angled stone design features were not incorporated within the Great Pyramid since they apparently resulted in premature dilapidation.

The final chosen design, of multiple horizontal courses of stone, varied in thicknesses; however, every block in each course was of a uniform height, and when laid on a stone foundation, was a close representation of a real mountain. Susceptibility to earthquakes was reduced and the sheer volume of stone with its steep sides made it almost impossible to ruin or disassemble.

Nonetheless, most casing stones from all three Giza pyramids were pilfered to construct later monuments and/or the early buildings of Cairo. The propensity of ancient cultures to destroy the monuments of prior cultures has always been a prime cause of destruction and although the outer white limestone casing of the Great Pyramid and the Pyramidian itself are gone, the basic immensity of the structure is still in place for all to see.

Entrance Door

The Entrance Door to the Great Pyramid internal structures and chambers (see Image 9.1) is located on the north façade, a little east (about 24 feet) of the north-south centerline of the structure and approximately 55 feet above the Courtyard level.

The reason this Phase 2 element is listed first chronologically is that the Descending Corridor* was begun by excavating a tunnel from the Giza Plateau surface to a level approximately 100 feet below the desert floor to allow the construction of the Subterranean Chamber*. Our theory suggests this was done to access the artesian aquifer that lay below the desert floor. Later, as the pyramid core blocks arose layer by layer, the stone courses extended the Descending Corridor* above the seventh layer, up to the Entrance Door. *Phase 1 Pyramid Elements*

Originally, the Entrance Door was said to have been protected by an enormous block of Tura limestone that matched the exterior cladding and rendered the exact location visibly imperceptible. This hidden entry door was allegedly balanced with extreme precision on pins that allowed the stone to act as its own counterweight, requiring only a slight pressure to activate and open, otherwise remaining tightly closed. This was the original Entrance that led immediately into the Descending Corridor* and down into the Subterranean Chamber*, both of which have been previously described in Chapter 4.

When the Caliph al-Ma'mun began his forced entry into the pyramid in the 9th century A.D., he began nearer the base and west of the actual location of the entrance. Reportedly, when his workers had tunneled a fair distance into the pyramid, they heard a loud rumble coming from a point further east of their location, and adjusting their vector to their perceived source of sound, they stumbled onto the Descending Corridor*.

Finding large red granite monoliths in the ceiling of the Descending Corridor*, they tunneled up and around the granite, ultimately finding their way into the Ascending Corridor and the mysteries that lay beyond.

The Entrance Door, other than providing workman entry during construction to the Ascending Corridor, Grand Gallery and working platforms up through the level of the King's Chamber, has no bearing on our construction theory.

Image 9.1 - The Original and Subsequent Entries into the Great Pyramid
Source: http://www.touregypt.net/featurestories/greatpyramid3.htm 1/31/2010

Ascending Corridor

The Ascending Corridor begins approximately 90 feet down the Descending Corridor* from the top of the pyramid Entrance Door. The Descending and Ascending Corridors in the Great Pyramid are stacked vertically, one above the other. The Ascending Corridor is noticeable from below in the Descending Corridor* ceiling by virtue of one of three pink granite monoliths set end to end, 7 tons each, which were placed in the Ascending Corridor to block the entrance where the two corridors meet (see Image 9.2); these granite plugs are still in place today. The Ascending Corridor branches off and upward at an angle of approximately 26 degrees, running for approximately 129 feet before reaching a junction with the Queen's Chamber Horizontal Corridor and the Grand Gallery. The Ascending Corridor is the same dimension as the Descending Corridor*, approximately 3 feet 9 inches high by 3 feet 5 inches wide.

* see Lower Pyramid Elements, Image 3.0

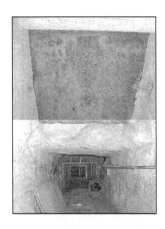

Image 9.2 - The Red Granite Plugs in the Ceiling of the Descending Corridor
Source: http://www.bibliotecapleyades.net/piramides/images/pyramid_003.jpg 2/23/2010

The Ascending Corridor (see Image 9.3) has three giant stones through which the corridor has been hewn, in donut fashion. These stones have been named "girdle stones" and are accompanied by an additional three "half-girdles" creating girdle stones that are actually two "U"-shaped stones joined together, all of which the corridor passes through. Much speculation has been offered for the presence and purpose of these stones; however, their presence, together with the Ascending Corridor itself, other than providing workman access, is not a part of our construction theory.

Image 9.3 - View of the Ascending Corridor to the Queen's Chamber Horizontal Corridor.
This view is looking up the Ascending Corridor and toward Grand Gallery.
Source: http://gizapyramid.com/newtour6.htm 4/30/2010

Queen's Chamber Horizontal Corridor

The Horizontal Corridor into the Queen's Chamber begins at the junction of the Grand Gallery's lower end, with the Ascending Corridor and extends approximately 150 feet in a southerly direction; it is approximately 3 feet, 6 inches wide by 4 feet high. At about 17 feet from the Queen's Chamber, the corridor floor suddenly drops down approximately 24 inches (see Image 9.4), and the remaining corridor makes its way towards the Queen's Chamber. We see no purpose this step may have had in the construction process.

Image 9.4 - View of the 24" step in the Horizontal Corridor to the Queen's Chamber. This view is looking back toward the Ascending Corridor and Grand Gallery. Source: http://gizapyramid.com/newtour6.htm 4/30/2010

Since the aforementioned corridors of the Great Pyramid are stacked vertically, one over the other and since the Grand Gallery slopes at the same angle as the Ascending Corridor, *the opening in the ceiling of the Horizontal Corridor to the Queen's Chamber is also the floor of the Grand Gallery* (see Image 9.5). It is believed that either there were wooden beams and planks sealing off the Horizontal Corridor from the Grand Gallery (Borchardt), or wooden beams supporting thick stone slabs were placed in the floor of the Grand Gallery (Dr. Lehner), separating it from the Horizontal Corridor servicing the Queen's Chamber.

At the beginning of the corridor where the Grand Gallery, Ascending Corridor and the Horizontal Corridor all converge, there is another element known as the Well Shaft. The Well Shaft is a vertical tunnel that runs through the core blocks, finally connecting with the Descending Corridor* just up from the Horizontal Corridor into the Subterranean Chamber*. The

upper opening to the Well Shaft is tucked into the sidewall, adjacent to, and opens into, the Horizontal Corridor to the Queen's Chamber.
see Lower Pyramid Elements, Image 3.0.

The stone slabs when present in the ceiling of the Horizontal Corridor, effectively separate the Horizontal Corridor to the Queen's Chamber from the Grand Gallery and Ascending Corridor. *This is an important element central to our theory of construction* that redirects the supply water from the Well Shaft into the Queen's Chamber and prevents it from draining down the Ascending Corridor into the Descending Corridor.

Image 9.5 The Junction of the Horizontal Corridor with the Grand Gallery. The square cut holes in the sidewalls were for beams that supported the thick stone floor slabs, now missing. The Queen's Chamber can be seen at the end of the Horizontal Corridor, below.
Source: http://www.touregypt.net/featurestories/greatpyramid3.htm 2/01/2010

Queen's Chamber

The Queen's Chamber is located at the 25th course of the pyramid core blocks and is oriented carefully on the pyramid's east-west centerline. It is approximately 19 feet long by 17 feet wide, and has gabled roof stones beginning their pitch at approximately 15 feet above the floor, extending to approximately 21 feet high (5.76 x 5.23 x 6.26 meters high). It is comprised of finished limestone blocks and has a corbelled vault forming a niche in the east wall approximately 15 feet high (see Image 9.6). The vault has been thought of as containing a statue and has no bearing on our theory of construction.

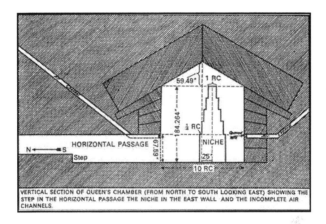

Image 9.6 Queen's Chamber
Source: http://www.guardians.net/egypt/pyramids/GreatPyramid.htm 3/9/2010

Although the room is called the Queen's Chamber, most experts agree that no Queen was ever interred there, but attribute use of the name to the gabled ceiling, a motif or shape apparently associated with female burial chambers in Ancient Egypt. In 1872, the Egyptologist Waynman Dixon, extrapolating from the "Ventilation Shafts" present in the King's Chamber, closely inspected the Queen's Chamber, hoping to find similar features. Inspecting around the walls of the Queen's Chamber in approximately the same relative location, some accounts have Dixon discovering a crack in a masonry joint in the south wall where he was able to insert a wire to a great length; others indicate that he was able to find the shafts by tapping on the stones until he heard a hollow sound (see Image 9.7).

Image 9.7 - View of the "Ventilation Shaft" in the Queen's Chamber.
Source: http://gizapyramid.com/newtour6.htm 4/30/2010

Dixon directed his assistant to probe a hole through the stone joints and found that after chipping away approximately 4-5 inches of stone thickness, the limestone was concealing "Ventilation Shafts" similar to those found in the King's Chamber. Some reports indicate that when the same thickness of stone was removed from the north shaft, a solid granite sphere, a double-tailed cast-copper hook and a 5-inch long slat of cedar-like wood were found (see Images 9.8 and 9.9). Actually, Dixon did not identify in which of the two lower shafts the relics were found, but mentions them in connection with the northern shaft. Apparently, the wooden slat had a cross-section of approximately 0.5 inch by 0.4 inch. [1]

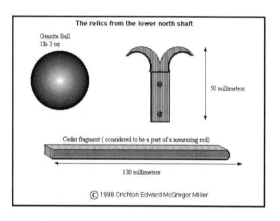

Image 9.8 - Drawing of the Granite Sphere & Copper Hook found by Waynman Dixon in the Queen's Chamber North Ventilation Shaft in 1872.
Source: http://www.crichtonmiller.com/the_dixon_relics.htm 2/2/2010

Image 9.9 - The Granite Sphere & Copper Hook found by Dixon in the Queen's Chamber North Ventilation Shaft in 1872.
Source: http://www.crichtonmiller.com/the_dixon_relics.htm 2/2/2010

In 1993, Rudolf Gantenbrink verified that the Queen's Chamber "Ventilation Shafts" do not extend through to the exterior of the pyramid, but instead are obstructed with fitted polished limestone blocks with two, either bronze or copper "L"-shaped handles, inserted into the face of each block. Also, the blocks appear to be held in place by vertical slots on both sides; the blocks are only approximately 5 millimeters wider than the shafts; the blocks appear to extend up through the shaft ceilings, but rest on top of the shaft floor (see Gantenbrink, www.cheops.org).

No visible trace of mortar is found on the blocks; this is unusual, since most blocks in the shafts do show such traces. The Gantenbrink team was able to recover bits of white gypsum mortar from the shaft, indicating as Gantenbrink states, *"...the shaft was indeed laid using mortar."* He goes on to say *"But the closure stone was apparently mounted with great precision and held in place by grooves or recesses, without using mortar. Thus, we may well assume that the stone is, in some way or another, moveable."* In support of our theory, we conclude that the blocks appear to have been designed as sliding doors, movable upwards (see explanation in the following King's Chamber section).

Image 9.10 - View of one of the blocks found in the "Ventilation Shafts" in the Queen's Chamber. Source: http://gizapyramid.com/newtour6.htm 4/30/2010

Recent photographic analysis seems to indicate the wall blocks in the Queen's Chamber containing the Ventilation Shafts appear to have been inset 4-5-inches back from the finished face of the chamber walls. A veneer block of 4-5-inches in thickness and of the same dimensions of the full block face was then fitted over the entire area of the inset block containing the shaft. The photo in Image 9.11 seems to reveal the presence of this veneer plate by the change in color of the plate versus the color of the shaft penetration itself through the primary block behind it.

Image 9.11 - View of the southern "Ventilation Shaft" in the Queen's Chamber.
Source: http://egyptologist.org/discus/messages/8/5603.html?1037295383 5/3/2010

Image 9.12 below, traces the location of the veneer plate and that of the primary shaft block behind it. This suggests that the Ventilation Shafts were put to a specific use and when having completed their utility, they were covered up having no further utilitarian, religious or spiritual purpose to the Ancient Egyptians.

Image 9.12 – Enhanced View of the southern "Ventilation Shaft" in the Queen's Chamber.
Source: http://egyptologist.org/discus/messages/8/5603.html?1037295383 5/3/2010

We believe the Ventilation Shafts servicing the Queen's Chamber were actually conduits, not for the soul, but for supply water to operate the Water Stairs for the upper reaches of Phase 2 of pyramid construction. In order to fuel the construction engine, supply water had to be provided above the working platform, at whatever level was under construction.

Evidence for the presence of water in the Queen's Chamber existed when it was first entered by modern expeditions; the walls were noted to have been encrusted with salt up to one-half to one inch in thickness.[2] The cause of this salt encrustation has heretofore been unsubstantiated. The salt encrustation was also noted to have been found in the Queen's Chamber Horizontal Corridor and the Subterranean Chamber all of which are locations where the supply water occurred. Unfortunately, the encrustations were apparently removed during a subsequent cleaning of the chambers.

Salt is plentiful in the Sahara Desert, the rock stratum having been laid under the saltwater seas to great depths prior to the collision of the continental plates that uplifted the northern portion of the African Continent (see Chapter 1). When exposed to water, the salt present in the Queen's Chamber limestone walls and core bocks over time would have leached out of the rock and been deposited upon the surface of the wetted chamber walls. This would be a process akin to the typical limestone cave formations found throughout the world and indeed, even below the Giza Plateau itself (see Chapters 1 and 2).

Additionally, the ceilings of the Ventilation Shafts are flush with the ceiling of the Horizontal Corridor to the Queen's Chamber. Since this corridor was the water supply conduit from the Well Shaft to the Queen's Chamber, it makes sense that their ceilings were constructed flush with one another. That way, water was drawn off the top of the Queen's Chamber reservoir at the point where the upper portion of the chamber would have resisted any further upward migration of water due to the air pressure contained within the top half of the Queen's Chamber. One of the peculiar characteristics of water is that it will always seek the path of least resistance. This trait would have redirected the water flow into the Ventilation Shafts on either side of the chamber, where the flow would continue its ascent.

Finally, the height at which the limestone blocks in the Ventilation Shafts are located above the desert floor sets them flush with the top corner of the bottom end of the top granite monoliths forming the roof of the King's Chamber. The significance of this aspect will be discussed in the King's Chamber section below.

Grand Gallery

The Grand Gallery begins at the junction of four disparate elements; the Ascending Corridor, the Horizontal Corridor into the Queen's Chamber, the Well Shaft/Grotto, and the Grand Gallery itself (see Image 9.13).

Image 9.13 The Junction of the Horizontal Corridor with the Grand Gallery. The Queen's Chamber can be seen at the end of the Horizontal Corridor, below. Source: http://www.touregypt.net/featurestories/greatpyramid3.htm 2/1/2010

The Grand Gallery is a tall, narrow and long void in the middle of the pyramid that slopes upward at the same angle as the preceding Ascending Corridor, approximately 26 degrees. It is comprised of seven courses of corbelled blocks of limestone, each overlapping the previous one by approximately 3-inches, to form a chapel-like or "A-frame" room that narrows at the top to approximately 41-inches wide. It is approximately 8.74 meters high by 2.10 meters wide by 47.85 meters long (28 x 7 x 158 feet long).

The Grand Gallery has a central passageway approximately two feet wide flanked by a narrow 18-inch ramp on each side. There are a series of square holes running along the ramps at regular intervals.

At the top of the Grand Gallery there is a large stone block that forms a step or platform approximately 3 feet high, 6 feet wide and 8 feet deep that functions as the threshold to the Horizontal Corridor that extends into the King's Chamber. Both the north (lower end) and south walls (upper end) of the Grand Gallery are also comprised of the same corbelled block technique that forms its long walls (see Image 9.14).

90

Image 9.14 – The Grand Gallery looking up toward the King's Chamber.
Source: http://www.bibliotecapleyades.net/piramides/pyramids/pyramids03.htm   2/23/2010

As previously stated, there is another element found at the beginning of the intersection of the Grand Gallery with the Horizontal Corridor to the Queen's Chamber, but located to the side in a niche of the corridor, known as the "Well Shaft", a hole approximately 3-feet in diameter that connects to the Descending Corridor near its intersection with the Horizontal Corridor to the Subterranean Chamber.

The Well Shaft could be considered a part of the Horizontal Corridor to the Queen's Chamber, as it would be separated from the Grand Gallery by the now missing stone slabs that formed a part of the Grand Gallery floor and/or the Horizontal Corridor ceiling, when in place. As mentioned above, *these slabs are critical to our theory,* in that their presence as floor slabs in the Grand Gallery floor, redirects the supply water flow to the Horizontal Corridor to the Queen's Chamber and ultimately to the Queen's Chamber itself.

As an interesting comparative juxtaposition, the Queen's Chamber veneer blocks or slabs were *installed after* completion of the monument to conceal the Ventilation Shafts, whereas the floor slabs in the Grand Gallery were *removed after* completion of the monument, to allow use of the Queen's Chamber for ritual purposes and provide foot traffic passage to and between

91

the King's and Queen's Chambers, as well as the Ascending and Descending Corridors and Entrance.

King's Chamber Horizontal Corridor

The step or platform threshold to the Horizontal Corridor leading to the King's Chamber gives way to a short passageway 41 inches square. About one-third the distance, or approximately 4 feet down the corridor, it widens into an Antechamber where all walls are now built of red granite, not limestone. The Antechamber is tall enough to stand up in, but measures only 21 inches front to back and about 42 inches side to side.

At this point, a granite slab or "leaf" about 16 inches in thickness, is suspended over the corridor. The leaf is comprised of two blocks, one above the other and they are suspended above the corridor in grooves in the sidewall; their bottom side is flush with the ceiling of the corridor. The remainder of the Antechamber is empty; by some reports, as many as three pink granite portcullis stones blocking the passage were supposed to have been suspended in place above the corridor by ropes over pulley-like wooden logs set into notches in the sidewalls. These blocks were presumably to be lowered into place to prevent entry into Khufu's burial chamber upon internment and completion; however, no traces of these blocks remain at this location.

After exiting the antechamber, another low corridor of about 8 feet in length is encountered before opening into the east end of the King's Chamber. The Horizontal Corridor to the King's Chamber does not enter into our theory of construction.

King's Chamber

The King's Chamber resides at the 50th course of the pyramid masonry and is approximately 35' long x 17' wide x 19' high (10.49 meters long x 5.42 meters wide x 5.84 meters high). It is comprised entirely of pink granite slabs, including the flat ceiling, which has 9 of the monoliths placed side by side with an estimated combined weight in excess of 400 tons. Above the ceiling slabs are a total of five so-called "Relieving Chambers", each approximately 2-3 feet high. Each chamber is separated from the next by the granite slabs forming its ceiling, as well as, the floor of the chamber above.

The lowest Relief Chamber was discovered in 1763 when Nathanial Davison found an entry hole about 24 inches wide, high up in the south wall of the Grand Gallery. Apparently, after cleaning away centuries of bat dung,

Davison crawled approximately 25 feet and found his way into a cavity that measured approximately 3 feet high and about the same length and width of the King's Chamber below. He observed that the floor he was on was comprised of 9 granite monoliths, each he estimated to weigh up to as much as 70 tons.

Later in 1837, Colonel Howard Vyse, discovered four subsequent higher relief chambers above the Davison Chamber. He noticed a crack in an end of one of the Davison Chamber ceiling slabs, probed the crack with a reed and was able to extend it approximately three feet. Anticipating another chamber above, Colonel Vyse forced entry into them by detonating gunpowder from within the Davison Chamber.

The side walls of the relieving chambers are comprised of both pink granite and limestone. Since the chambers were never meant to be entered after construction, graffiti found in them by Colonel Howard Vyse, including the cartouches of both Khufu and his co-regent Khafre, represent the best evidence for the pyramid to have been associated with the Pharaoh Khufu.

From the floor to the top of the top chamber, the King's Chamber measures approximately 20.7 meters high (69 feet). One of the few signs of subsidence of any sort having occurred in the Great Pyramid is evidenced by that crack in one of the Davison Chamber ceiling monoliths, at the south end.

As discussed above in the Queen Chamber's section, the top corner of the bottom end of the granite monoliths forming the top peak of the King's Chamber roof are at the same height and nearly flush with the limestone blocks in the Ventilation Shafts servicing the Queen's Chamber. *This is the point in Phase 2 Construction of our theory where the remaining monoliths in the Font Pond were unloaded from their barges and placed in their pre-determined locations in the King's Chamber roof* (see Image 9.15).

The significance of this relationship may be due to the realities of unloading a 70-ton monolith from a floating barge to the adjacent working platform in preparation for its incorporation into the monument.

We theorize that if the limestone blocks in the Queen's Chamber Ventilation Shafts actually functioned as check valves do in today's plumbing systems, then being able to raise or lower the water level in the Font Pond in very small increments to level the bottom of the monoliths' wooden sledges with the working platform surface would have greatly facilitated unloading the massive monoliths, by simply sliding them off the wooden runners of the barge, onto the limestone working platform of the pyramid made perfectly flush by adjusting the water level in the Font Pond.

This of course provides a reason and accounts for the Ventilation Shaft blocks or "doors" having been set into channels chiseled into the shaft sidewalls; they move upwards. Although there is not much clearance from the top of the copper handles set in the door to the top of the shaft ceiling, it appears that approximately 2-3 inches of clearance would have been gained from the bottom of the shaft door to the floor of the shaft. Fully retracted, each shaft would still have provided a supply water "pipe" of approximately 2-3 inches by 8 inches.

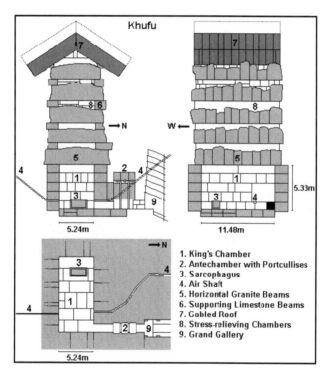

Image 9.15 The Kings Chamber – Three Views
Source: http://www.unexplained-mysteries.com/forum/index.php?showtopic=128645 3/9/2010

This is approximately double the size of pipe we calculated in Appendix A.12, which was based on providing 22 cubic feet per minute or 164 US gallons per minute. Also see in Appendix A.13, where this rate of water delivery represents a pipe three to four inches in diameter. Remember, this was the size of pipe required to effectively supply all the water needed to deliver the total stone payload in the pyramid within the 20-year historical timeframe.

From the working platform, the roof slabs would have been ushered into position and guided into place with the aid of temporary wood false-work beams braced to the structure.

The King's Chamber also has the so-called "Ventilation Shafts", located in a similar fashion to their counterparts in the Queen's Chamber (see Image 9.16). However, there is one significant difference in these shafts…they extend all the way through the pyramid and exit through the casing stones to the atmosphere. There is evidence to indicate they were at one time outfitted with hinged iron doors, perhaps gold plated, near where the shafts penetrated the casing stones, at approximately 234 feet and 175 feet, above the desert floor (found by Colonel Howard Vyse, in 1837).

Image 9.16 – View of the typical "Ventilation Shaft" in the King's Chamber.
Source: http://gizapyramid.com/newtour6.htm 4/30/2010

The northern shaft is approximately 5 inches high x 7 inches wide, is approximately 235 feet in length and slopes at angle of approximately 31 degrees. The southern shaft is approximately 8 inches high x 12 inches wide, is approximately 175 feet in length and slopes at angle of approximately 45 degrees.

The King's Chamber Ventilation Shafts have historically been considered to have been the transport conduit of the King's soul on its journey to the heavens; the King's Chamber and its Ventilation Shafts have no function in our construction theory.

1. "Grant Bey And The Missing Pyramid Relic Carbon 14 Dating The Great Pyramid Continued", © Robert G. Bauval 2002, Published in Discussions in Egyptology, Oxford, Volume 50, 2001.

2. Smyth, Charles Piazzi, "Life and Work at the Great Pyramid", Volume II, page 56.

Note: A significant amount of material, text, photos and illustrations for this Chapter was taken directly from articles written for the website Tour Egypt by the author Alan Winston.
Source: http://www.touregypt.net/featurestories/greatpyramid3.htm 2/01/2010

Note: Additional material for this section was taken from the article, "A Deep Look of the Great Giza Pyramid" found at the following website:
Source: http://www.bibliotecapleyades.net/piramides/pyramids/pyramids03.htm 6/02/2010

Chapter 10 – Pyramidian and Final Finishing

Pyramidian

Among the myriad of technical issues to be addressed is the placement of the capstone, or Pyramidian. This stone, as its name implies, is a perfect pyramid unto itself and is situated at the top of the monument; it is the final course of stone to be placed. Its size can only be estimated, since no remnant has ever been recovered and at least two or more of the top courses of core blocks are missing as well. However, other Pyramidians have been recovered in whole or in pieces, reassembled and can be utilized for comparative purposes and extrapolated to the conditions prevalent at the Great Pyramid.

One thing is certain though, the Pyramidian stone reached the top of the edifice by means of the Water Stairs. The "Font Pond" envisioned for the large monolithic stones had been retired and filled in with core blocks through the utilization of the principle of displacement, after the last roof monolith of the King's Chamber had been set, a couple of hundred feet below the pinnacle. By virtue of its design, the square footage of the pyramid working platform continued to diminish at each level. At the very top, the Pyramidian stone replaced the final floor area or footprint available, with a single pointed stone; a perfect pyramid itself, the zenith or pinnacle of the entire construction.

Pyramidian Size

The actual physical size of the Pyramidian was limited by the capacity of the Water Stairs used to transport it to the top and the ability of the workers to manhandle it from the topmost Water Stair into its position at the peak. This means that the Pyramidian dimensions would have been dictated by the same volume (weight) limits as the other stones.

If the Water Stair limit of 1 cubic meter of stone was used, the maximum Pyramidian could have been 1.64 meters square at the base and 0.68 meters tall (65 inches square by 27 inches high). This is unlikely in our estimation due to the resulting weight of 2,600 Kg. (5,700 lbs.).

More than likely, the Pyramidian was sized similarly to the thickness of the adjacent coursework which averaged about 22 inches at the upper courses. This calculates to a Pyramidian of approximately 34 inches square at the base and 22 inches high weighing 371 Kg, or 818 lbs. A Pyramidian of this size would still require use of the Water Stairs.

At the level of the smallest platform the Egyptians felt they needed in order to function, the Pyramidian was delivered by the water stairs. Probably, from that point upward, a single Water Stair was maintained to deliver the Pyramidian to the very top. At probably the third to last course, the last core block was placed, whereas, the second to last course was probably comprised of only the four cornerstones that ultimately supported the Pyramidian itself.

The Great Pyramid's Pyramidian was most likely beveled on its bottom surface, fashioned to a convex profile to fit into its natural counterpart, a concave surface fashioned on the four cornerstones immediately below it. This was a measure calculated to ensure that it was not subsequently dislodged by a seismic or windstorm event.

This method was recently reported by Dr. Hawass to have been used on the satellite pyramid of Khufu (G1-d), one of the adjacent Queen's Pyramids. A portion of the third course below the apex for this pyramid was found on the south side of the pyramid and was built of the same fine Tura limestone as the Great Pyramid. The stone still had three of the four exterior sloped faces intact and comprised more than one-half of the south side of the third course.

Dr. Hawass writes, *"...the underside of this block was flat but the top surface was shaped as a concavity."* Also, *"This concavity of the top surface was intended to receive the convex underside of the block(s) forming the second course down from the top. The block or blocks of the second course down from the top are missing, but later we found that actual apex stone of the satellite pyramid, a single piece of fine Tura-quality limestone. The underside of the pyramidian was convex, with four triangular faces sloping outward 7.3° to (sic) the center point of the base. This protruding convex base was meant to fit into the concavity of the second course from the top, just as the blocks of the second course had evidently fit into the convex (sic) top surface of the third course down."* [1]

Alternatively, the four corner stones could have been milled to form a socket for a Pyramidian that had a tenon, or a projecting pin or rod of stone that fit into the socket, but with room for movement, for even greater resistance to potential movement, similar to each of the four foundation corner stones at the base of the structure.

Final Working Platform

Since the footprint of available work area was rapidly diminishing with the completion of each course, the Egyptians realized they would soon run out of room to facilitate construction operations. So with several courses to go, perhaps as many as seven, the Ancient Egyptians probably erected a platform of cedar wood near the top of the pyramid.

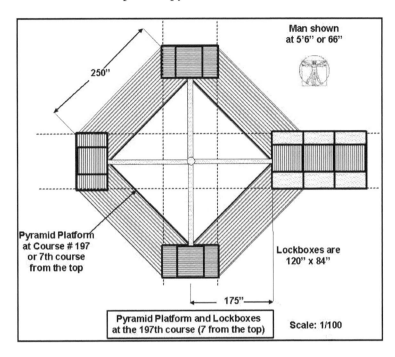

Image 10.1 Possible working platform at 7 courses below the pinnacle
Source: The Authors

It would have been tied to and interlaced with the Water Stairs at each of the four corners and braced to the faces of the pyramid between the corners. This would have afforded them a mobilization area sufficient to negotiate activities related to the placement of the remaining stones.

However, the cornerstones were not yet in place beneath the Water Stairs. Remember that Herodotus stated that the elder priests told him that the pyramid was completed from the top down. *"The upper portion of the pyramid was finished first, then the middle, and finally the part which was lowest and nearest the ground."* Egyptologists have historically interpreted this to mean the casing stones were either placed after the core blocks had been placed, or were finished in place after the last stone was located.

Casing Stones

We postulate that the casing blocks that sheathed the pyramid in a brilliant white polished Tura limestone, contrary to mainstream Egyptology, were placed in finished condition as the pyramid was being erected. It is difficult to imagine how any other method, secondary or duplicative, would have been employed to hoist these stones into place after the core blocks were in place. It is also difficult, if not impossible, to imagine that the ancients planned to finish or polish the casing stones after they were set in place.

Such a concept would have made it very difficult to line up the blocks during placement, since the face required to be lined up would have been hidden by superfluous rock still a part of the casing stones. Sight lines would have been required to be set up and maintained throughout the construction phase, above the actual height of the finished face of the pyramid to account for the stone not yet removed. The final face would then have been derived by a series of plumb bobs dropped from a temporary line established in the work area, and flushed with the sight line above it (see Image 10.2).

Image 10.2 Pyramid of Unas casing blocks 09/06/2009
Source:http://4.bp.blogspot.com/_c1QyoNpgQxU/RpM
upUEJ8I/AAAAAAAABCU/RRO6jsqqZPQ/s1600/saqqara_unas02.jpg

The difficulty of perfectly milling the face of the pyramid from top to bottom by beginning to chisel away at the top and continuing down to the bottom while standing on the course immediately below is further compounded by having to concurrently match the efforts of the workmen on the other three adjacent faces. During that process, any rock surface errantly removed by incorrect alignment could have never been rectified, since millions of pounds of stone had already been placed above it. Any replacement of errant stonework would not have been possible or would have only allowed a superficial fix at best. How then, was it done?

Prefabricated Construction

A process of construction that is currently and commonly employed worldwide involves the placement or incorporation of individually pre-manufactured components of a building in a pre-determined manner. Component parts are manufactured, numbered, shipped to the site in final form and assembled in place; each piece is directed to its predetermined location, placed, then plumbed and adjusted to the adjacent parts and to the whole structure concurrently. This type of construction is known as prefabricated, or pre-cast in the case of concrete, or panelized in the case of masonry, stone or metal panels, and is commonly employed for placing the glass and metal or stone facing panels on the steel superstructures of high-rise buildings.

Each panel is lifted into place by mechanical means, usually a hydraulic or cable-traction crane lift, and bolted to the building frame through use of a steel sub-girt system that attaches to the back of the panels and to the structural frame, and is adjusted for alignment both vertically and horizontally and for depth, by slotted steel angles, then finally permanently bolted or welded into place. Transits are employed to determine the final placement of each piece to ensure each manufactured piece is aligned with the other adjacent components and to the structure as a whole. Taken incrementally, this process is very exacting and can be seen taking place today on high rise structures worldwide.

Evidence of prefabricated construction being employed in Ancient Egypt is documented in many of the country's most famous landmarks, including the Great Pyramid. Both component numbers and manufacturer's or crew's trademarks have been found on the backside of individual stones and monoliths incorporated in many of the country's monuments; both the Pharaoh's cartouche and crew's names have been found in the Great Pyramid and confirm that the ancients were custom crafting individual components offsite, to be incorporated within the edifice at predetermined locations. The work crews each had a name and their names have been found along with leveling lines recorded with red iron oxide paint on the sides of a few of the casing stones and in the King's Chamber. The numerical markings and the use of specially crafted monoliths indicate that at least some of the stones were destined for an exact spot in the building.

Extrapolating that historic information together with that of our current construction technologies, we can conclude that, in all likelihood, all the important stones contained within the Great Pyramid including all the casing stones, were pre-milled in the quarry to exact specifications and tolerances, loaded onto their individual sledges, tied on with ropes, shipped to the jobsite, directed to their final and specific location within the pyramid, and aligned with the adjacent stones already there and with the entire edifice as a whole.

While the limestone core blocks could have been, and apparently were, much less exacting in their measurements and fit, the casing blocks were meticulously milled and set one to the other with great precision. We believe this was done by creating multiple wooden jigs which were dispersed among all quarrymen and used to create the exacting tolerances needed at standing joints and to effect the 52 degree exterior slope of the pyramid face; these jigs could quickly reveal high spots in the stone surfaces while still at the quarry allowing for the pre-finishing of each and every casing stone to perfection. This especially includes the cornerstones at the four spines or "Arrises" of the pyramid from top to bottom.

However, one very important difference is that, while all the casing stones and the giant monoliths within the various chambers of the pyramid were incorporated when construction had reached their level, the cornerstones above the seventh course were not. This was because the Water Stairs, used for conveying 84 percent, more or less, of the stones used in the construction, were employed at and occupied the corners of the pyramid, thereby necessitating the later inclusion of the cornerstones. This is the reason that the priests that Herodotus interviewed some 2,500 years ago, held that the pyramid *was finished from the top down!*

Cornerstones

How is it possible that, while all the stones of the Great Pyramid were placed as construction advanced upward, the cornerstones could be placed after the fact? One of the peculiarities of stone is that it has great strength in compression, but relatively little in tension. That is to say, while a stone can resist great pressures from loading weight onto the top of it, when stone is used as a spanning member, where it functions as a lintel, it is very brittle and will break into two pieces when comparatively little weight is superimposed upon it.

This is due to its low resistivity to bending or tensile forces. Said another way, while it is very difficult to crush stone, it is a comparatively easy task to break it. As a result of the physical characteristics of stone, it will not deflect when it is cantilevered; that is to say, it will not easily or readily bend when loaded, but instead will reach a point quickly in its capabilities to resist a load in tension, and then will suddenly snap into two pieces.

When unloaded, a small piece of stone cantilevered beyond the point of bearing will remain rigid and exhibit no distortion in bending. Therefore, a cornerstone perfectly milled to the requirements of its neighboring stones, can be slid into place under the cornerstone piece located immediately above it, without fear of its binding on a stone deflecting above it.

Owing to the perfection of milling by the ancient stonemasons, each cornerstone would be delivered to its respective course by the Water Stairs, where it would be prepared with a slip of gypsum mortar on all sides, top and bottom, and then glided off its wooden sledge and into place. That level of Water Stair, or lockbox, would then be dismantled and the next opening prepared to receive the next cornerstone below it. In this manner, *it would appear to any observer standing on the plateau, that the pyramid was finished from the top down!*

It should be understood here that the area of bearing for each cornerstone was taken primarily by the core block immediately below it within the pyramid. With the exception of the Pyramidian, the cornerstones do not bear upon the cornerstone immediately below. The area where cornerstones touch one another lies within the cantilevered area only (see Image 10.3) and because the stones do not deflect in bending, they only come into contact by virtue of the thin layer of gypsum mortar between them.

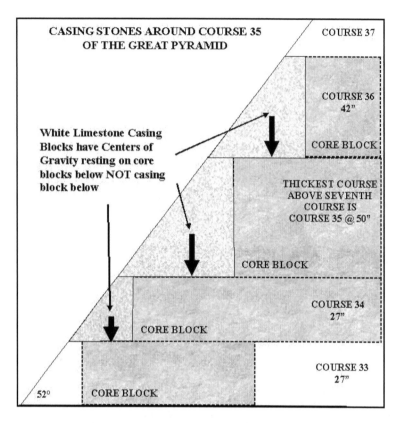

Image 10.3 Casing blocks resting on core blocks below
Source: The Authors

This process would have continued, one step at a time downward, until the top of the seventh course was reached, where Phase 1 construction was completed by virtue of the Enclosure Pond contained by the Enclosure Wall, previously discussed.

As a further insight to the placement of the casing and cornerstones, remember that the pyramid of Khafre still has its casing stones intact at the very top of the pyramid. If these stones relied primarily on the lower casing stones for support they would have fallen long ago. The fact that they remain in place today gives credulity to our conclusion about their method of assembly and support.

1. Studies in Honor of William Kelly Simpson, Volume 1
Department of Ancient Egyptian, Nubian, and Near Eastern Art
Museum of Fine Arts, Boston 1996
Copyright Museum of Fine Arts, Boston 1996
The Discovery of the Satellite Pyramid of Khufu (GI–d), by Dr. Zahi Hawass, pages 385 and 386

Chapter 11 – Phase 2 Water Flow

Upward Flow

In our method of construction, beginning with the first course, the artesian well water from the Well Shaft would be contained to fill a Font Pond, which rose inside the footprint of the pyramid with each successive working level of the pyramid. The Font Pond would have had no valves or gates to control the water flow, as the flow would have been continuous into each of the supply pipes (or channels) that supplied the Water Stairs above the seventh course at each of the four corners. The supply pipe would have also functioned to allow the continuous flow of supply water to bypass the Water Stairs, but the supply pipe would have been fitted with a connection and valve to the top portion of each Water Stair lockbox to raise the water level in each box on command.

In addition, a waste pipe would have paralleled the supply pipe and would have connected to the bottom of each Water Stair lockbox, also with a valve, to allow the lowering of the water level within each lockbox and would have redirected the waste water directly into the Enclosure Pond below. In this manner, the system would have prevented any flooding or overflow conditions from occurring and given autonomy of operation to the operators of any of the lockboxes at any given time. There would have been water valves at the Mortuary Temple (Lock #1) to control the level of the water in the Enclosure Pond and an overflow to allow water to escape through the lower locks and eventually into the Nile.

Three Water Stairs were able to provide a steady supply of individual casing stones and core blocks to each subsequent level of construction. Blocks would have been off-loaded onto the course under construction, would have glided across the stone platform of the course below on their individual sledges, been lowered to the surface, then the blocks could have been slid into position. Sledges would have been returned to the Enclosure Pond by the fourth Water Stairs and sent back to the quarries to begin another cycle.

At the same time as it was supplying the Water Stairs, the Font Pond continued to be supplied by the Well Shaft with water to raise the monolith-carrying barges one level at a time. When the Font Pond was established at the first course, since the Grotto was already located near the top of the limestone outcropping at the summit of the Giza Plateau, it was by necessity placed adjacent to the mound. As the first seven courses were erected, the Font Pond was moved sideways, incrementally with each successive course, until it was directly superimposed over the artesian Well and Grotto. In this manner the massive stone monoliths were simply floated to their respective locations, fed by the artesian well, extended upwards by the Well Shaft and Font Pond, high above the desert floor, where they were ultimately off-loaded at their respective levels of incorporation.

As the pyramid construction rose to the top of the seventh course, about 26 feet above the pyramid base, the construction of the Ascending Corridor was begun in a southerly direction, while the Descending Corridor was continued up at the same angle in a northerly direction towards the north face of the pyramid. Both shafts appeared as simple openings in the working platform until the construction continued up to about 55 feet above the pyramid base (the 13th course level of stones) where the Descending Corridor exited the north face of the pyramid and terminated in an archway, which was effectively hidden by the pivoting stone door at the Entrance. The Font Pond continued its independent march up the pyramid nearby, with each successive lift of the masonry courses.

The Ascending Corridor construction continued up several more stone courses, to a point where it intersected with the Well Shaft, Horizontal Corridor to the Queen's Chamber, and the bottom of the Grand Gallery. The builders did not want water to flow into the Grand Gallery, or to flow back down the Ascending Corridor, so they diverted the well water down the Horizontal Corridor toward the Queen's Chamber, and into the Font Pond, which by this time, had been moved closer to the center of the pyramid.

This action would allow any astronomical activities that may have been taking place in the Grand Gallery to continue uninterrupted and would have allowed workmen access into the Grand Gallery and the working platform, through the main Entrance, without having to climb the Water Stair staircases.

As the Font Pond was raised higher with each course of the pyramid, it continued to supply water to the balance of the pyramid construction. When the Font Pond got to the level of the Queen's Chamber floor, the well water, in seeking its potentiometric height (see Image 1.4), would continue to rise from the top of the Well Shaft and flow into and along the Horizontal Corridor toward the Queen's Chamber. *The water was diverted into the Horizontal Corridor by the now missing stone slabs in the Grand Gallery floor.*

Concurrently, the builders began constructing the Queen's Chamber within the Font Pond. The reason for this is because the Queen's Chamber was now

106

part of the supply water delivery system; the supply water was to be diverted from the Well Shaft into the Queen's Chamber where the Ventilation Shafts would allow its continuing upward journey.

When the water level was flush with the level of the ceiling of the Horizontal Corridor, it was also flush with the ceiling of the Ventilation Shafts in the Queen's Chamber. This provided a water supply that allowed construction to continue upward until the Queen's Chamber was completed.

Once the Queen's Chamber roof monoliths were in place, the supply water with nowhere else to escape, would flow up the shafts to feed working water into the Font Pond holding the monolith barges, which now were at a level higher than the Queen's Chamber roof.

As previously stated (see Queen's and King's Chambers, Chapter 9), the Ventilation Shafts have blocks or doors in them that are coincident in elevation with the top corner of the bottom end of the granite monoliths of the King's Chamber roof (see Image 9.15). *We believe these blocks/doors are actually sliding doors that allowed the workers to control the level of water in the Font Pond, which facilitated the critical off-loading of the huge roof monoliths.*

In our theory, at this point all the monoliths had been unloaded from their barges and incorporated in their permanent locations within the monument. The Font Pond was then retired, filled in with core blocks and the supply water from the Well Shaft was redirected by the Ventilation Shafts towards the arrises, or corners of the pyramid, for continued use by the Water Stairs. After the monoliths were placed, the boats or barges carrying them were dismantled and returned via the Water Stairs to the Enclosure Pond and through the locks, then out into the Nile.

Above the level of the top of the King's Chamber, we have no information on the water delivery system within the pyramid. The Ventilation Shafts from the King's Chamber exited the side of the pyramid, were open to the King's Chamber interior and were never considered to have held water, as no salt encrustation has been found above the Queen's Chamber.

The shafts from the Queen's Chamber slope upwards and outwards to almost the side of the pyramid at their known extremity. *No exploration of the Ventilation Shafts has occurred beyond the second door of either shaft* (at the time of this writing, August 2010, Dr. Hawass has scheduled another probe of the shafts and intends to drill through the second door). If extensions of these shafts are ever found, due to their proximity to the exterior face of the pyramid, we believe they would have been directed inwards towards the center of the pyramid under construction (see Image 11.1). We postulate they came together at the center of the pyramid to flow upward in one vertical shaft almost to the top of the pyramid or at least to the last working Water Stair. Mr. Samuel Laboy, a Civil Engineer from Puerto Rico, who has done extensive geometric analysis and calculation of the internal elements of the Great Pyramid indicates that any extension of the Ventilation Shafts beyond the second limestone doors as we have suggested, would be approximately 197.60 feet long culminating at the proposed vertical shaft that runs to the top of the pyramid (personal correspondence); many other configurations were possible.

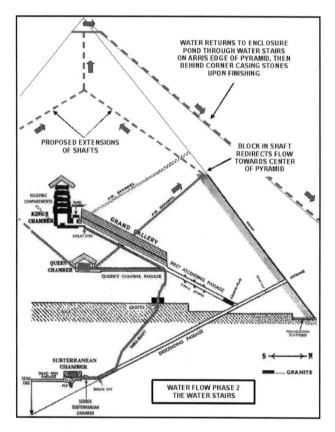

Image 11.1 Phase 2 Water Flow – Source: The Authors

At least one of the Water Stairs was probably built to the top to facilitate the off-loading of the Pyramidian, the perfect pyramid capstone at the pinnacle of the monument. Probably the four cornerstones supporting the Pyramidian, at the second to last course, were brought up to their level by their respective

108

Water Stair lock boxes. The size of the Water Stair lock boxes, based on their required water capacity to function, would have touched each other at the top of the third course from the top. This means that each of the cornerstones would have been off-loaded directly, from its respective lockbox, into position to comprise the second course from the top. The Pyramidian would then be transported to its final destination by one lockbox that extended up to the top course.

Downward Flow

With the upward journey of the pyramid construction complete, what remained was the insertion of each casing cornerstone below the second course from the top, a task that repeated itself all the way down each of the arrises, until the seventh course of the pyramid where the first lock box was constructed. In order for that to happen, each lock box still required a water supply to deliver each cornerstone up to its respective level in the pyramid.

Since the water flow had reached its maximum height at the bottom of the second course from the top, it had to be redirected to each arris in order to provide the necessary flow to the Water Stairs to deliver each subsequent cornerstone on the way down. We posit that this was done by creating a horizontal channel or trough cut into the bottom of each casing cornerstone and vertically into the back of each casing cornerstone (see Image 11.2), to form channels that conducted the water. In this manner, the water flow was now directed downward, in stair-step fashion.

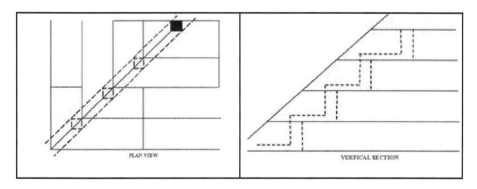

Image 11.2 Channels/troughs cut into Core Blocks behind Cornerstones – Source: The Authors

It is likely, as the core blocks were set, on the way up the masons applied a thin gypsum mortar coating to the exposed core block faces abutting the cornerstone channels, rendering them virtually watertight. Later, when used as a part of the downward supply water conduit assembly, the loss of water to leakage through the core blocks was eliminated. Each cornerstone was slid off its sledge directly into position and the water flow behind it was automatically diverted to the next course below and returned to the supply pipe, where it made its way into the adjacent Water Stair lock box, Enclosure Pond, Mortuary Temple lock, Causeway, Valley Temple lock and finally, into the River Nile.

Stopping the Flow

Once the monument was completed, the problem of stopping the flow of the artesian well had to be confronted. This was because the Queen's Chamber would not be able to be used for ritual services due to the presence of water up to the height of the top of the Ventilation Shafts and filling the Horizontal Corridor.

There are several opportunities to do this, the first one being at the well source in the Subterranean Chamber. There does not appear to have ever been a blocking stone present in the chamber; besides, the chamber would have to have been accessed in order to achieve plugging the well. In accessing the chamber, the water pressure and level from the active well would have made its plugging difficult, if not impossible.

The next opportunity would have occurred at the juncture of the Well Shaft and the Descending Corridor. We believe that a stone wall existed at one time just up the Descending Corridor from the penetration into the Well Shaft, that diverted the water flow into the Well Shaft and kept it from extending up the Descending Corridor; *it should be noted that we are unable to find any evidence of such a wall thus far.*

However, Dr. Mark Lehner says that in 1817, when Giovanni Battista Caviglia cleared the Descending Corridor, he had to dig out about 200 feet of rubble to get to the Well Shaft. No other details of this excavation are given, but Dr. Lehner goes on to say that Caviglia also went on to find the Subterranean Chamber, presumably clearing his way into it as well. Any remnants of the wall that may have existed to direct the water flow into the Well Shaft certainly would have sustained major damage or even total destruction in the clearing process. However, prior to Caviglia's efforts, the Caliph al-Ma'mun was also purported to have been into the Subterranean Chamber in the 9th century A.D. and could have initially damaged or destroyed any such wall in his quest for treasure, but no detailed records of this intrusion have been found. Nonetheless, the same problem would have

110

confronted the builders at this location as that they faced in accessing the Subterranean Chamber, when determining how best to plug the well.

Therefore, the third opportunity presented itself in the Grotto where there is an unexplained large red granite monolith laying just to the side of the Well Shaft proper, between the shaft and the enlarged chamber of the Grotto. This monolith apparently has a hole bored through it and may have been designed to act as a plug to staunch the flow, but for some reason, appears to have never been employed for that purpose. Others think that this monolith is one of those missing portcullis stones used to block entry into the King's Chamber, although how it got there is difficult to understand. Since the water flow would have fully submerged this area anyhow, the same problem that confronted the builders at the first two opportunities was also present at this location.

This brings us to perhaps the best opportunity for plugging the Well Shaft and shutting down the source of the construction engine for the project. That opportunity was presented to the builders by the removable stone planks in the Grand Gallery floor. Remember that in our theory, the Grand Gallery and the Ascending Corridor were kept dry in order to provide easy access to the Grand Gallery for alleged astronomical activities, and to the working platform for on-going construction activities.

This feature forced the supply water into the Queen's Chamber and up the Ventilation Shafts. Since the Well Shaft intersected with the Horizontal Corridor at the junction of the Grand Gallery and Ascending Corridor, all that had to be done was to remove the stone slabs in the Grand Gallery floor. Then a stone plug could be inserted into the top of the Well Shaft in the niche, or sidewall, of the Horizontal Corridor to the Queen's Chamber. Any water that spilled into the Grand Gallery in the process would have drained down the Ascending Corridor where it could have been quickly mopped up. The amount of water that may have spilled would have been negligible, since the operation would have been quick to complete.

This solution would have left the Well Shaft full of water, but with no outlet, it would have stopped the flow of water upwards completely. Since the Well Shaft and the Subterranean Chamber did not need to be accessed for ritual purposes, the project was complete and the construction engine was shut down.

Remnants of Flow

Over time, with the climatological changes already at hand during the Old Kingdom in Ancient Egypt, the water would have eventually receded all the way back down the Well Shaft, the Descending Corridor, the Subterranean Chamber itself and finally, to the Pit or Well that tapped the artesian aquifer that lay beneath the Giza Plateau. When earnest exploration of the monument began, the water was long since gone and only the remnants of any such presence would have remained. This probably accounts for the heavily eroded nature of the Subterranean Chamber, Well Shaft itself, and the Ventilation Shafts, not to mention the presence of the ½ to 1 inch thick encrustation of salt on the walls of the Queen's Chamber, the Horizontal Corridor to it, a small amount that apparently leached into the bottom of the Grand Gallery and the Subterranean Chamber.

One final aspect remains to be determined regarding the water flow at the Great Pyramid. We believe that the Pharaoh and his entourage probably visited the pyramid complex for periodic rituals and festivals while still alive. What better way for a king to arrive at his monument than as Pharaoh floating on his throne in his sun barque, the first in a flotilla of craft accessing the pyramid complex by means of the Valley Temple lock, Causeway, Pyramid Temple lock, and finally the Enclosure Pond? When arriving at the Enclosure Pond, the Pharaoh was ferried around to the north side where the pyramid Entrance was situated and since the freeboard of his barque probably elevated the Pharaoh to around 30-35 feet or so above the courtyard level, he needed only to ascend the final 20 feet or so to the hinged Entrance stone. This could have been done by a wooden staircase affixed to his barque that when extended to the face of the pyramid, allowed the Pharaoh and his priests to gracefully disembark into the depths of his pyramid to the afterlife beyond.

Since the water flow had been stopped within the monument when the construction engine was shut down, in order to supply a continuous flow to replenish the Enclosure Pond and supply the Causeway, a second source of water had to be tapped. We have no information on a second well that supplied the Enclosure Pond, Causeway and locks, but feel there is a good chance that one existed; alternatively, sufficient water flow could have been provided to the Enclosure Pond courtyard by an existing natural fissure in the bedrock, of which there were at least two known. The entire history, religion, mythology and creation story of Ancient Egypt is replete with images of water, boats, and the primordial mound. The image of the pyramid as Ben-Ben stone emerging from the abysmal void would have been apropos

112

and the epitome of their statement of pyramid as resurrection machine and the site of rebirth of the Pharaoh.

After the Pharaoh's death, the Valley and Mortuary Temples were then completed and since trips to the tomb for rebirth and funerary practice were no longer needed, the water delivery system was rendered obsolete, and with the climatic changes already upon the Giza Plateau, arid conditions then prevailed upon the site.

End of Phase 2 Construction

Chapter 12 – Levels of Evidence

We believe that there is a wealth of evidence supporting our findings and theory. It is comprised of a "boat-load" of circumstantial and physical evidence, as well as, a surprising amount of historical evidence. We believe that, due to the overwhelming amount of circumstantial evidence and to the lesser amount of historical evidence, there is justification enough to validate our theory.

However, the significant amount of physical evidence that we have found thus far correlates so well with the other evidence, that taken as a whole, we believe that it may be time for reconsideration and reinterpretation of certain specific physical features still in place at the Great Pyramid. Whether these features will ultimately prove to be the "smoking gun" overlooked by the enquiring minds of archaeologists, Egyptologists and pyramid enthusiasts worldwide or not, will determine whether the theory itself is greater than the sum of its parts.

To recap, we have proposed a hydrological construction method that utilizes the conditions prevalent at the Giza Plateau during the Fourth Dynasty of the Old Kingdom of Ancient Egypt. We believe this method, or one very similar to it, was used to build the first and longest lasting of the original Seven Wonders of the World.

We have shown that a fantastic powerhouse of energy was available to the Ancient Egyptians in the form of an artesian well that tapped into the aquifers that lay under the Sahara Desert by means of the well dug at the bottom of the Subterranean Chamber.

We have found a use and explanation for the existence of the Well Shaft that conducted the confined waters from the base of the Descending Corridor to the Horizontal Corridor into the Queen's Chamber.

We have shown how that water was distributed by means of the so-called "Ventilation Shafts" to greater heights within the pyramid that continuously fed a "Font Pond" at the top of the working platform of the level under construction.

We have indicated that the water supply was then directed from the "Font Pond" to the four corners of the pyramid to provide the continuous water supply needed to power the "Water Stairs" and how the Water Stairs lifted the core blocks and casing stones up to each subsequent level under construction.

We have shown how the "Font Pond" was constructed concurrently with the first course at the pyramid base in order to create a central pond that housed the giant monoliths on their individual barges that were later to be incorporated in the Queen's Chamber, Grand Gallery and King's Chamber by the principle of displacement and how the Font Pond was raised incrementally with each level of the pyramid construction.

We have shown how the Water Stairs extended from the top of the seventh course to the very top of the pyramid in order to place the Pyramidian stone and how the Enclosure Pond received the water from the Water Stairs and held a reservoir of water to aid in minimizing the level changes when the Mortuary Temple lock was activated.

We have shown how the supply water was diverted to the arrises for its stair-step return trip through the pyramid itself and by the supply pipe and Water Stairs that allowed conveyance and placement of each cornerstone and the return of the supply water to the locks and ultimately, the River Nile below.

Finally, we have shown how the Causeway was a series of water locks that allowed the transport of all of the stones from the Nile River to the building site and the supply water, from the artesian well, located in the Subterranean Chamber, to flow into the River Nile.

Following is a listing of that evidence, by category, relevant to the proposed delivery methods employed by the Ancient Egyptians, offering proof of our theory:

Circumstantial

1. Ancient Egyptians were accomplished Hydrologists with an extensive history of well drilling and water management.
2. Ancient Egyptians were accomplished Seamen, Stevedores and Longshoremen.
3. Ancient Egyptians were accomplished Quarrymen, Stone Masons and Surveyors.
4. Ancient Egyptians were accomplished Boat Builders and Carpenters.
5. The Fourth Dynasty of Ancient Egypt followed a long period of equatorial monsoons that provided and replenished the aquifers annually.

116

6. The monsoons of the Equatorial Highlands had begun to abate by the First Dynasty (3,100 BCE) and the region entered a protracted drought. It would have taken many years for the drought to have negatively affected the enormous artesian aquifer, but it had certainly taken place by the end of the Fourth Dynasty (2,600 BCE).

7. At the beginning of the Fourth Dynasty, the Sahara Desert began a period of intense desertification that continues unabated to the present day.

8. The end of the Fourth Dynasty coincides with the end of the 100-year history or so, of large stone pyramid construction; therefore, the construction engine that fueled the process expired and could no longer be used.

9. The Giza Plateau had an existing artesian well at the site of the Grotto and also 300-feet to the south of the Sphinx's right paw and remnants of both remain today.

10. Projected cross-sectional analysis of the remaining foundation stones of the Enclosure Wall correlate with the structural profile of a retaining wall.

11. We have computed the Ventilation Shafts were of sufficient cross-sectional area to deliver the required water flow to render the Water Stairs operational.

12. We have computed the Water Stairs cross-sectional area and size are sufficient to deliver the blocks to the top.

13. We have computed the Enclosure Pond was of sufficient cross-sectional area and volume required to provide the flow of water needed to operate the Causeway lock system.

14. The Valley Temple was built in a location that allowed stone transport at the lowest river levels, while being submerged during the annual Nile inundation.

15. The construction method delivers blocks to the top of the working platform at a rate that would comply with or hasten the historical construction period of approximately 20 years. All four corners or "Arrises" of the pyramid would have had water stairs, with three of them delivering stones and the fourth returning the sledges to the base of the pyramid. This means that instead of delivering one block per increment of time, the Water Stairs would deliver three.

Historical

1. The delivery method uses a machine built of short wooden planks, one for each level of construction, per the "Histories" of Herodotus.

2. The delivery method accounts for the pyramid being completed from the top down, per the "Histories" of Herodotus.
3. The delivery method presents a rational reason or justification for the discontinuance of large stone pyramids after the Fourth Dynasty due to drought conditions in the equatorial highlands and desertification of the Sahara Desert.
4. The delivery method described incorporates well known Ancient Egyptian technologies.
5. The delivery method provides an explanation for the salt encrustations that were encountered in the Horizontal Corridor to the Queen's Chamber, the Queen's Chamber itself, the bottom of the Grand Gallery and the Subterranean Chamber.

Physical

1. Stone sockets in the foundation of Causeways of the same period have been found that indicate the use and location of heavy wooden doors with metal pin hinges in the exact spot you would expect them to occur when functioning as lock gates.
2. There is a well in the Subterranean Chamber that extends at least 12-feet and perhaps as much as 60-feet down.
3. There are signs of heavy erosion on the floor and walls in the Subterranean Chamber.
4. There is a Well Shaft in the pyramid that also appears to be heavily eroded; it connects the Descending Corridor near the Subterranean Chamber to the point in the Queen Chamber's Horizontal Corridor where the Ascending Corridor, Grand Gallery, and the Horizontal Corridor all converge.
5. There are slots in the sidewall of the Horizontal Corridor to the Queen's Chamber that are thought to have supported wooden beams of sufficient capacity to support the thick stone floor slabs of the Grand Gallery, now missing. These slabs would have redirected the supply water into the Queen's Chamber and kept it from entering the Grand Gallery and Ascending Corridor.
6. The ceiling of the Horizontal Corridor into the Queen's Chamber is flush with the ceiling of the Ventilation Shafts that redirect the water upwards.
7. A ½ -1" thick salt encrustation was found in the Queen's Chamber and remarked on by Petrie; the encrustation was limited to the Queen's Chamber, the Horizontal Corridor to the chamber, and the Subterranean Chamber, with a small amount reported in the bottom of the Grand Gallery, probably from leakage.

8. There are two limestone blocks in the southern Queen's Chamber Ventilation Shaft and at least one in the northern shaft; both front blocks have "L"-shaped copper/bronze arms or handles protruding from the face of the blocks. The blocks sit on the top of the floor, but are set into sidewall channels. The top of the blocks appear to extend up and beyond the ceiling of the shafts. The southern shaft has a second block approximately 20 cm. beyond the first. The blocks may have moved vertically in the manner of a sliding sluice gate or door.

9. The limestone blocks in both Ventilation Shafts are nearly flush with the top corner of the bottom end of the top granite monoliths forming the roof of the King's Chamber. Functioning as check valves, the doors at this placement would have allowed sensitive adjustment of the supply water flow into the Font Pond during the off-loading of these largest monoliths from their barges, perhaps critical to their movement onto the construction platform.

10. There is a Grotto near the location where the Well Shaft exits the live rock. The Grotto appears to have been partially improved with rock masonry and the circumference expanded in the manner of public water wells, indicating the possible long-term presence of the well on the Giza Plateau.

11. There are at least two natural fissures in the bedrock that were probably a part of the fault in the formation that created the ancient natural artesian well present at the Giza Plateau.

12. If the remaining casing stones at the top of the adjacent pyramid of Khafre can be extrapolated to the Great Pyramid, it is indicative that the casing stones center of gravity is located above the core block below and not the casing stone below it (see Image 10.3). This supports our hypothesis that the casing stones were placed level by level and that the corner casing stones could have been installed from the top down.

13. There was an Enclosure Wall surrounding the pyramid. The wall has been estimated at approximately 26-feet tall which would provide an Enclosure Pond with depth sufficient to have handled the delivery of all monoliths, core blocks and casing stones. Recent revisions to the estimate (Dr. Lehner) of the wall height put it at 10-feet high; this is still high enough to provide the required water depth for all stone delivery.

14. There was a Causeway that could have provided water access to the Enclosure Pond year around and would have been sufficiently large to deliver all stones into the Enclosure Pond.

15. The Ventilation Shafts in the Queen's Chamber have been thought to have been wrought from a single large block with the shafts

terminating approximately 4-5-inches behind the finished face of the chamber walls. Recent analysis suggests that a full-size stone block veneer panel 4-5-inches thick was placed over the shaft block that was inset by 4-5-inches. This suggests a utilitarian use for the shafts, specifically for the delivery of supply water for construction, that upon completion, were no longer needed and which were subsequently covered up.

16. The floor planks in the floor of the Grand Gallery, which double as ceiling planks in the Horizontal Corridor to the Queen's Chamber, are missing, probably as a result of their having been removed after construction to allow re-entry into the Queen's Chamber for ritual purposes and to access the niche in the Horizontal Corridor to the Queen's Chamber to plug the water flow from the Well Shaft.

17. Director of the Egyptian Supreme Council of Antiquities, Dr. Zahi Hawass has said the copper handles on the Ventilation Shaft blocks/doors bear the sign of the work gang "The Green Ones" and probably the hieroglyph "prjj", which means "to come out". Dr. Hawass has interpreted this to reference the transport of the soul, but it could be referring to the supply water instead.

Implications

1. The end of the Fourth Dynasty coincided with the end of the 100-year history or so, of large stone pyramid construction. The implication is that a protracted drought would have ultimately diluted the strength of an aquifer-based construction delivery system that relied on artesian water power, rendering the system obsolete. Historians and archaeologists have consistently indicated that the end of large stone pyramid construction was due to drought conditions that impacted the Egyptian wheat harvest that then reduced the country's financial resources to the point where the state could no longer afford to build such expensive construction projects.

2. The construction method delivers blocks to the top of the working platform at a rate that would comply with or shorten the historical construction period of approximately 20 years. All four corners or "arrises" of the pyramid would have had water stairs, with three of them delivering stones and the fourth returning the sledges to the Enclosure Pond at the base of the pyramid. This means that the construction period required to deliver the stones could approach as much as one-third of that possible with any other theory proposed to date; this of course assumes that sufficient blocks could be quarried

and delivered by river at the rate needed to support the anticipated improvement in erection speed.

3. This construction technique could sufficiently shorten the duration of construction time required for all large stone pyramids and makes sense of the notion that all large stone pyramids were completed within a roughly 100-year or so, time span.

Occam's Razor

This principle is attributed to a 14th century English logician, theologian and Franciscan friar, William of Ockham. The maxim holds that *"...entities must not be multiplied beyond necessity"*, with the conclusory result that, the simplest solution is usually the correct one. Further, when competing hypotheses are equal in other respects, the principle recommends selection of the hypothesis that introduces the fewest assumptions and postulates the fewest entities while still sufficiently answering the question.

We believe that our theory makes the fewest assumptions of any theories proposed thus far concerning the construction of the Great Pyramid or the capabilities of the Ancient Egyptians. We also believe that our theory provides a measure of empirical evidence lacking in other methods with which we are familiar.

Franz Lohner in his website, Building the Great Pyramid (www.cheops-pyramide.ch), has stated that there are at least five requirements that every pyramid construction theory should fulfill:

1. *A solution that is as simple as possible using a technology that is as simple as possible (Occam's razor)*
2. *Continuity in technical matters and craftsmanship.*
3. *Verification through pictures and/or text.*
4. *Technology keeping with the time and culture.*
5. *The supposed technique/method must really be a solution.*

What could be simpler than building a confining structure around an artesian water source to harness its lifting powers? Such a system was merely an extension of the technologies that the Ancient Egyptians had long-since mastered as hydrologists managing their agricultural and maritime needs. We have no need for elaborate rope and quasi-pulley arrangements; nor do we need thousands of workers muscling huge payloads up steep ramps or steeper pyramid slopes. We have no treacherous corners perched hundreds of feet above the desert floor, around which to negotiate the monoliths. Their boat building and irrigation talents were simply applied to the task at hand.

The continuity of their technologies is apparent in applying their expertise in maritime activities and irrigation farming to the problem of the vertical placement of stones. They clearly had the craftsmen to build the Water Stairs in the manner in which they built their boats. No new technical matters had to be invented; existing technologies were just applied to new problems.

Above we have compiled a list of 15 points of circumstantial evidence, 5 points of historical evidence, and 17 points of physical evidence that supply sufficient verification of our theory and have documented them with photos, drawings, examples and text in the preceding chapters.

We have pointed out the technologies used by the Ancient Egyptians had already been under their employ, likely for centuries preceding the construction of the Great Pyramid.

Finally, we have presented a fully integrated solution for the construction of the Great Pyramid that solves the most menacing problems faced by the Ancient Egyptians and the Egyptologists. *We have tested our theory against the built monument as it exists today and found an existing and accommodating feature of the pyramid just where it is needed to facilitate the concept.* Among others, our delivery method details how the largest monoliths were effortlessly delivered to their level of incorporation, hundreds of feet above the desert floor; *we are unaware of any solution proposed to date that presents a believable method for doing that.* We have done so with a method that mirrors what was reported by Herodotus; one that employs the use of *"...machines made of short wooden planks."* We have also finished the pyramid in Herodotus' words, *"...from the top down".*

We believe that given a similar site with similar conditions, restrictions and resources to those the River Nile and the Pharaoh Khufu possessed at the Giza Plateau in the Old Dynasty, we could complete the same project today. The reason is because we have seen all the various technologies we have described here at work in our own lifetimes.

The Ancient Egyptians were equally adept on land or at sea. They already possessed the technologies needed for the project and called upon their various experts to bring their expertise to bear on the solution together. They were blessed with their unique location on the banks of the River Nile, whose northerly flow could be navigated upstream by wind, affording travel in both directions. The presence of the great artesian aquifers underlying the west bank of the River Nile during the Old Kingdom was serendipitous in the extreme and powered the engine that made possible the construction of the first and only remaining Wonder of the World, the Great Pyramid of Giza.

End

APPENDICES

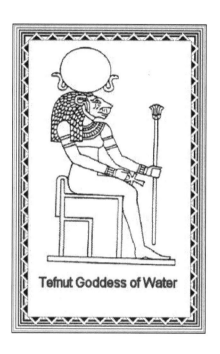

Tefnut Goddess of Water

A.1 - Darcy's Law application

In Chapter 1 we discussed how an artesian well can be formed when rainwater trapped between two impermeable layers escapes to the surface through faults in the underlying rock. The flow rate of an artesian well can be determined by applying Darcy's Law.

In his book *"Elements of Physical Hydrology"* Section 6.3, George M. Hornberger discusses Darcy's Law. In 1856 the French hydrology engineer Henry Darcy published an equation for flow through a porous medium that today bears his name:

$$Q = \frac{KA\ h_1\text{-}h_2}{L}$$

Where Q is the total discharge through the aquifer, A is the cross sectional area modified by a constant K, which is a measure of the permeability of the rock stratum, h_1 is the elevation of the recharge zone, h_2 is the elevation at the flowing artesian well and L is the distance between them.

Unfortunately we could find no information on Q, K or A, for our subterranean aquifer and we doubt that the data exists, but we do have data for h_1 (the height of the recharge area in the Ethiopian Mountains) and, h_2 (the height of the top of the Great Pyramid at Giza) and L (the distance between them).

The average elevation of the Ethiopian Plateau is about 1,680 m (about 5,500 ft) and the elevation of the base of the GP is about 60m above sea level (Giza Survey). The height of the GP is reported to be 146 m (481 ft) so the elevation of the top of the GP is about 60 + 146 = 206 m. The distance from the Ethiopian Plateau to Giza (Cairo) is about 2,600 km so Darcy's Law begins to look like this ... Q = KA x (1,680 – 206)/2,600,000 or Q = KA x 0.0006.

In Appendix 12 we have calculated the amount of water flow to raise the GP in 20 years at 22 cu ft per minute (0.623 m^3 per minute). Let's be generous and choose a flow rate of Q = 3 m^3 per minute and see how big KA has to be to balance the equation.

So Q or 3 = KA x 0.0006, so KA = 5,000 m^2 (say 100 m x 50 m) which is obviously much smaller than the actual cross section of the permeable rock stratum available at the Giza Plateau.

A.2 – Sahara desertification

Sahara's Abrupt Desertification Started By Changes in Earth's Orbit, Accelerated By Atmospheric and Vegetation Feedbacks

Science Daily (July 12, 1999) — WASHINGTON -- One of the most striking climate changes of the past 11,000 years caused the abrupt desertification of the Saharan and Arabia regions midway through that period. The resulting loss of the Sahara to agricultural pursuits may be an important reason that civilizations were founded along the valleys of the Nile, the Tigris, and the Euphrates. German scientists, employing a new climate system model, have concluded that this desertification was initiated by subtle changes in the Earth's orbit and strongly amplified by resulting atmospheric and vegetation feedbacks in the subtropics. The timing of this transition was, they report, mainly governed by a global interplay among atmosphere, ocean, sea ice, and vegetation. Their research is published in the July 15 issue of Geophysical Research Letters.

The researchers, headed by Martin Claussen of the Potsdam-Institut fuer Klimafolgenforschung (Potsdam Institute for Climate Impact Research) employed a model of intermediate complexity to analyze climate feedbacks during the past several thousand years of the current, or Holocene, era. Called CLIMBER-2 (for CLIMate and BiosphERe, version 2.1), the model led to the conclusion that the desertification of North Africa began abruptly 5,440 years ago (+/- 30 years). Before that time, the Sahara was covered by annual grasses and low shrubs, as evidenced by fossilized pollen.

The transition to today's arid climate was not gradual, but occurred in two specific episodes. The first, which was less severe, occurred between 6,700 and 5,500 years ago. The second, which was brutal, lasted from 4,000 to 3,600 years ago. Summer temperatures increased sharply, and precipitation decreased, according to carbon-14 dating. This event devastated ancient civilizations and their socio-economic systems.

The change from the mid-Holocene climate to that of today was initiated by changes in the Earth's orbit and the tilt of Earth's axis. Some 9,000 years ago, Earth's tilt was 24.14 degrees, as compared with the current 23.45 degrees, and perihelion, the point in the Earth's orbit that is closest to the Sun, occurred at the end of July, as compared with early January now. At that time, the Northern Hemisphere received more summer sunlight, which amplified the African and Indian summer monsoon.

128

The changes in Earth's orbit occurred gradually, however, whereas the evolution of North Africa's climate and vegetation were abrupt. Claussen and his colleagues believe that various feedback mechanisms within Earth's climate system amplified and modified the effects touched off by the orbital changes. By modeling the impact of climate, oceans, and vegetation both separately and in various combinations, the researchers concluded that oceans played only a minor role in the Sahara's desertification.

The CLIMBER-2 models showed that feedbacks within the climate and vegetation systems were the major cause of Saharan desertification, building rapidly upon the effects of the initial orbital changes. The model suggests that land use practices of humans who lived in and cultivated the Sahara, were not significant causes of the desertification. Further investigation is necessary, the researchers say, to determine more precisely the specific effects of latitude and oceanic feedback, as compared with biospheric feedback, on the timing of the event.

A.3 – More on Sahara Desertification

Uncovering Secrets of the Sphinx, by Evan Hadingham, Smithsonian, (February 2010 Volume 40, Number 11). Excerpt from pages 40 and 41: **Emphases** *by Sampson & Read.*

The Sahara has not always been a wilderness of sand dunes. German climatologists Rudolph Kuper and Stefan Kröpelin, analyzing the radiocarbon dates of archaeological sites, recently concluded that the region's prevailing climate pattern changed around 8,500 B.C., with the monsoon rains that covered the tropics moving north. The desert sands sprouted rolling grasslands punctuated by verdant valleys, prompting people to begin settling the region in 7,000 B.C. Kuper and Kröpelin say this green Sahara came to an end between 3,500 B.C. and 1,500 B.C., when the monsoon belt returned to the tropics and the desert reemerged. That date range is 500 years later than prevailing theories had suggested.

Further studies led by Kröpelin revealed that the return to a desert climate was a gradual process spanning centuries. This transitional period was characterized by cycles of ever-decreasing rains and extended dry spells. Support for this theory can be found in recent research conducted by Judith Bunbury, a geologist at the University of Cambridge. After studying sediment samples in the Nile Valley, **she concluded that climate change in the Giza region began early in the Old Kingdom with desert sands arriving in force late in the era.**

The work helps explain some of Lehner's [Dr. Mark Lehner] findings. His investigations at the Lost City revealed that the site had eroded dramatically – with some structures reduced to ankle level over a period of three to four centuries after their construction. "So, I had this realization," he says, "Oh my God, this buzz saw that cut our site down is probably what also eroded the Sphinx." In his view of the patterns of erosion on the Sphinx, intermittent wet periods dissolved salt deposits in the limestone, which crystallized on the surface, causing softer stone to crumple while harder layers formed large flakes that would be blown away by desert winds. The Sphinx, Lehner says, was subjected to constant "scouring" during this transitional era of climate change.

"It's a theory in progress," Says Lehner. "If I'm right, this episode could represent **a kind of 'tipping point' between different climate states – from the wetter conditions of Khufu and Khafre's era to a much drier environment in the last centuries of the Old Kingdom.**"

The implication is that the Sphinx and the **pyramids, epic feats of engineering and architecture, were built at the end of a special time of more dependable rainfall,** when pharaohs could marshal labor forces on an epic scale. But then, over the centuries, the landscape dried out and harvests grew more precarious. The pharaoh's central authority gradually weakened, allowing provincial officials to assert themselves – culminating in an era of civil war.

Today, the Sphinx is still eroding. Three years ago, Egyptian authorities learned that sewage dumped in a nearby canal was **causing a rise in the local water table.** Moisture was drawn up into the body of the Sphinx and large flakes of limestone were peeling off the statue.

Dr. Zahi Hawass arranged for workers to drill test holes in the bedrock around the Sphinx. They found **the water table was only 15 feet beneath the statue.** Pumps have been installed nearby to divert the groundwater. So far, so good! "Never say to anyone that we saved the Sphinx," he says. "The Sphinx is the oldest patient in the world. All of us have to dedicate our lives to nursing the Sphinx all the time."

130

A.4 - Murals of stone transportation

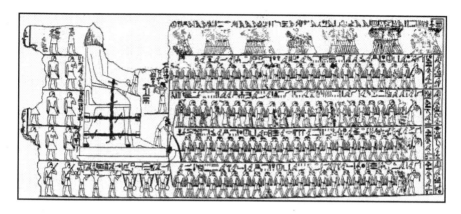

Mural of Djehutihotep's Statue being dragged in 12th Dynasty Egypt
Source: http://www.catchpenny.org/movebig.html 3/22/2010

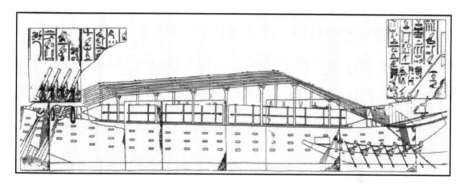

Hatshepsut's obelisk barge in 18th Dynasty
Source: http://www.catchpenny.org/movebig.html 3/22/2010

Oxen pulling stone on sled from painting 1000 years after Khufu
Source: www.cheops-pyramide.ch/.../ramp-models.html 3/20/2010

A.5 – Average weight of the 2.3 million stones

We have read often in books that it took approximately 20 years to build the Great Pyramid and that it contains 2.3 million stones averaging 2.5 tons in weight. We have never seen any corroborative methodology that determines these numbers, so we will try to derive some of our own numbers and compare them with the above.

From our Appendix A.12 we found the volume of the GP is approximately 92 million cubic feet (2.6 million cubic meters).

Limestone weighs 2,611 kilograms per cubic meter therefore the GP weighs 2.6 million, times 2,611 kg = 6,788,600,000 kg, or times 2.2046 lb = 14,966,140,000 lbs. Thus the GP weighed 6.79 billion Kg or 14.97 billion lbs in its completed state.

If there were 2.3 million stones they would weigh on average 6.79 billion kg / 2.3 million = 2,952 Kg or 2.952 metric tons each. Alternatively, 14.97 billion pounds divided by 2.3 million, which is 6,508 pounds, which is 3.25 short tons or 2.91 long tons.

There are three types of tons. The metric ton is 1,000 kilograms. The Avoirdupois short ton is 2,000 pounds and the Avoirdupois long ton is 2,240 pounds. The short ton will be ignored for this exercise, so we get the average weight of stones is 2.95 metric tons or 2.91 long tons.

Conclusion: **It appears that the often stated average weight of each of the 2.3 million stones is closer to 2.9 tons than 2.5 tons.**

However, the 2.3 million stones number does not take into account the many voids in the pyramid, such as the chambers, shafts and corridors, so the actual number of stones will be less and so would the total weight, since the weight calculation assumes a pyramid with no voids.

A.6 – Were there 2.3 Million stones in the Great Pyramid?

We have never seen a derivation of the 2.3 million stones number, so we will attempt to approximate the number of stones in the Great Pyramid, ignoring the previously mentioned voids.

The thicknesses of the courses vary considerably. According to Lemesurier there are 203 courses plus the missing capstone or pyramidian. Judging from

132

the course thickness chart in Appendix A.13, the average thickness of courses 1 through 106 is about 35 inches, and courses 107 through 203 average about 23 inches thick. To check this estimate against the height of the pyramid let's add them up.

106 x 35" = 3,710 inches or 309.17 feet, plus 96 x 23" = 2,208 inches or184.00 feet which add up to 493.17 feet which is 12.17 feet higher than the GP at 481 feet. So, let's adjust down the estimated average thicknesses to 34 inches and 22 inches and compute again.

106 x 34" = 3,604 inches or 300.33 feet, plus 96 x 22" = 2,112 inches or 176 feet which totals 476 feet or 5 feet short of the GP's 481 feet ... close enough for this estimate and the missing 5 feet is probably close to the height of the missing capstone and its supporting stones.

We now have a virtual pyramid with the lower 106 courses 34 inches thick and the upper 96 courses 22 inches thick. Unfortunately the length and depth of each stone is random so we will have to again estimate an average stone profile to estimate a number of stones.

Starting with the 34 inch stones, assuming a cubic profile the volume of stone would be 39,304 cubic inches or 22.75 cu ft or 0.644 cubic meters. With the 22 inch stone, assuming a cubic profile, the volume of stone is 10,648 cubic inches or 6.16 cubic feet or 0.174 cubic meters.

Now we have a virtual pyramid with the lower portion consisting of 106 courses of 34 inch stones and an upper portion consisting of 96 courses of 22 inch stones. The volume of the upper portion is equal to the area of the base times the height divided by 3. In a right pyramid the base length is proportional to the height, so the base of the upper portion of the pyramid is 176 x 756/481 = 276.62 feet. Thus the volume of the upper portion of the virtual pyramid is 276.62 x 276.62 x 176/3 = 4,489,093 cubic feet or 127,134 cubic meters.

Subtracting this from the previously determined GP volume of 92 million cubic feet (2.6 million cubic meters) we get the volume of the lower portion of the virtual pyramid at 87,510,907 cubic feet and 2,472,866 cubic meters. Now we can estimate the number of stones in the lower portion at 2,472,866/0.644 = 3,839,854 stones. The number of stones in the upper portion at 127,134/0.174 = 730,655 stones.

The above estimates the total number of cubic stones to be 3,839,854 + 730,655 = 4,570,509, much larger than 2.3 million, meaning the lower stones must have had a much larger profile (volume) than a cube of 0.644 cubic meters, and the upper stones must have had a much larger profile (volume) than a cube of 0.174 cubic meters.

To arrive at 2.3 million stones the stone volumes used above would have to be 4,570,509/2,300,000 or 1.99 times larger than a cubic profile. Hence a 22 inch stone would have to be 22" x 22" x 44" and a 34 inch stone would have to be 34" x 34" x 68" or some combination of depth and length that created a volume 1.99 times the cubic profile.

Conclusion: **Since the size and profile of the stones varied so much, the number of stones is indeterminate (as Petrie's measurements confirmed, see Chapter 2, The Quarries) and could amount to well over 2.3 million!**

A.7 – Volume of stone in the first seven courses

We need to know the volume of the bottom 26 feet 7 inches (26.58 feet) of the pyramid, which is the volume of the first seven courses. One way to do that is to calculate the volume of the shorter pyramid shape (above the seventh course) and subtract it from the whole. We have already calculated the volume of the whole Great Pyramid at about 92 million cubic feet (26 million cubic meters).

The height of the upper pyramid is $481 - 26.58 = 454.42$ feet. The length of the side will be less than 756 feet by an amount slightly less than twice 26.58 (due to the slope of the pyramid face at ~52 degrees). The arc tangent of 52 degrees is 1.2799 so the baseline will be shortened by 2 x 26.58/1.2799 = 41.53. The side of the upper pyramid is now 756-41.53 = 714.47. The volume of the upper pyramid is 1/3 x 714.47 x 714.47 x 454.42 = 77,322,196 cubic feet.

The above calculations do not take into account the fact that the pyramid base contains a natural rock outcrop, which would tend to decrease the amount of imported stones.

Conclusion: The amount of stone in the first seven courses (92 – 77.32 million cu. ft) = 14.68 million cu. ft or about 16% of the whole pyramid.

A.8 – Pyramid dimensions used in calculations

Height including capstone   481 feet
Length of sides   756 feet
Face Angle   ~52 degrees
Edge (Arris) angle   ~42 degrees

A.9 - To find the angle of the "arris" edge of the pyramid

Pyramid base is 756 x 756 feet.
Diagonal of base is therefore is the square root of $(756)^2 + (756)^2 = 1,069.15$ (checked by scale drawing). Half of this diagonal is $1,069.15 / 2 = 534.57$.

Drawing is a <u>diagonal</u> cross section of pyramid. To find the angle to the horizontal...

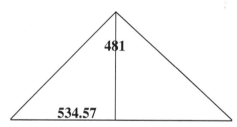

Tangent of this angle is 481/534.57 or 0.8998 or **41 degrees 55 minutes.**
Piazzi Smyth computed this angle at 41degrees 58 minutes

A.10 - Metric conversions

1 meter   = 3.28 feet
1 Square meter   = 10.76 square feet
1 kilometer   = 0.62 miles
1 Cubic meter   = 35.31 cubic feet
1 kilogram   = 2.2046 lbs
1 Cubic foot   = 7.481 US gallons

A.11 - Stone/water density

Granite weighs   2,691 Kg/cu meter
Limestone weighs   2,611 Kg/cu meter
Sandstone weighs   2,323 Kg/cu meter
Water weighs   1,000 Kg/cu meter
Water weighs   62.43 lbs/cu ft

A.12 – Volume of water required to float the Great Pyramid

Our theory suggests that the Great Pyramid (GP) was built using the lifting power of water. The following is an attempt to determine how much water would be required to float all the stones in the GP.

Volume of the GP = 1/3 x base area x height
= 1/3 x 756ft x 756 ft x 481 ft (original size with limestone casing)
= 1/3 x 274,908,816 cu ft
= 91,636,272 cu ft of stone *(2,595,193 cu meters)*

Limestone is 2.611 times the density of water (see A.11 above). So the volume of water required to balance this amount of stone would be approximately 2.611 times the volume of stone.

= 91,636,272 cu ft x 2.611
= 239,262,306 cu ft *(6,776,049 cu meters)*

According to historical assumptions the GP was built in approximately 20 years, therefore we can determine what delivery rate of water was required.

239,262,306 / 20 = 11,963,115 cu ft per year
11,963,115 / 365 = 32,775 cu ft per day
32,775 / 24 = 1,366 cu ft per hour
1,366 / 60 = 22.76 cu ft per minute (164 gallons per minute)

A small flowing artesian well could produce this amount of water. This represents a pipe 3-4 inches in diameter (see Appendix A.13).

Conclusion: In order to float the Great Pyramid it would require displacing 6.7 million cubic meters of water. This volume of water would be equal to water flowing at 22.76 cubic feet per minute (164 gallons per minute) for 20 years.

A.13 - Water flow capacities of pipes

Maximum water flow capacity of steel pipes - dimensions 2 - 24 inches

Pipe Size (inch)	Maximum Flow (gal/min)	Velocity (ft/s)	Head Loss (ft/100ft)
2	45	4.3	3.9
2 1/2	75	5.0	4.1
3	130	5.6	3.9
4	260	6.6	4.0
6	800	8.9	4.0
8	1,600	10.3	3.8
10	3,000	12.2	4.0
12	4,700	13.4	4.0
14	6,000	14.2	4.0
16	8,000	14.5	3.5
18	10,000	14.3	3.0
20	12,000	13.8	2.4
24	18,000	14.4	2.1

Source: http://www.engineeringtoolbox.com/steel-pipes-flow-capacities-d_640.html

From the above table a steel (or copper) pipe between 3 and 4 inches diameter could deliver 164 gals per minute.

A.14 - Artesian Wells and Flow Rates

It is difficult to ascertain what the water flow from the Giza well may have been so we sought information on general artesian well flows. We found a paper, Technical Fact Sheet SJ2001-FS3 issued in 1998 by the St. Johns River Valley Water Management District in Florida.

Source: http://sjr.state.fl.us/technicalreports/pdfs/FS/fs_artwells98.pdf

This is the northern part of the Florida Atlantic Coast. The paper was a result from their Abandoned Artesian Well Plugging Program, which was a water conservation program. In fiscal year 1997-98 a total of 128 wells were plugged or repaired saving an estimated 34.91 million gallons per day, which averages to a flow rate of 272,734 gallons per well per day. There are 7.48

US gallons per cubic foot, so this represents 36,462 cubic feet per day, or 1,519 cubic feet per hour or 25.32 cubic feet per minute ... very close to our required flow rate of 22 cu. ft/min from the Giza artesian well, which we derived in Appendix A.12.

Another interesting piece of well flow rate information is from the Edwards Aquifer in San Antonio, Texas.

"San Antonio [Texas, USA] began to rely on artesian wells for its water supply in 1891. These are two of San Antonio's first municipal water supply wells. The photo shows the tremendous amount of pressure that Aquifer water was under at that time. If we estimate the two men in the photo to be around 5 1/2 feet tall, then the column of water shooting up from the well is around 25 feet high! The effect of releasing all this pressure through wells was that spring flows began to decline immediately and significantly. By 1896 there were approximately 40 wells in the San Antonio area. By around 1900 San Antonio Springs had been reduced to just a trickle in most years.

This photograph [below] appeared in R. T. Hill & T. W. Vaughan's 1896 report on the geology and underground waters of the Edwards Plateau. Hill and Vaughan were the first geologists to recognize that wells such as these had impacted spring flows. They were the first people to accurately describe the Edwards and how it works. Although they never used the word 'aquifer', they referred to the Edwards as an artesian groundwater system, accurately described the catchment and transmission of water in the Aquifer, and recognized its large extent from Brackettville to Austin.

Artesian well in San Antonio, circa 1895
http://www.edwardsaquifer.net/intro.html

They even accurately predicted the existence of the large contiguous artesian zone between San Antonio and Del Rio in which good water can be obtained anywhere. Before their publication, the widely held belief was that waters supplying the artesian wells and spring rivers in south Texas came from the distant Rocky Mountains. They recognized that was impossible, and they explained the true source is the rainfall of the Edwards Plateau."

A.15 – Float/Lock Box/Water Stair size requirements

The pyramid builders must have made a determination as to the maximum volume (weight) of a stone to be raised in the Water Stairs. Those of the thicker course heights would have smaller depths and lengths to stay within the volume limit. It can be seen in the photo of the Great Pyramid below the variety of stone dimensions, even within the same course. It is likely that each Water Stair was made a standard size and the support structure custom fit on every one or more courses.

Stone size variability - Climbing the Great Pyramid.
Photograph by J. Pascal Sébah, about 1880.

The thickest block above the 7th course (other than the unknown pyramidian) was course #35 at 127 cm or 50 inches. The vast majority of the course thicknesses were less than 35 inches up to course 105. From course 106 (top of the King's Chamber Ventilation Shafts) upwards the majority of the course thicknesses were less than 23 inches. Whereas each course had a uniform block thickness (height) the other two dimensions of the blocks (depth and length) varied randomly.

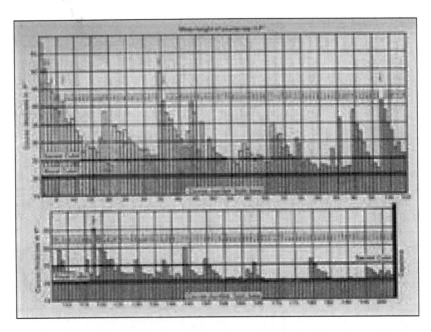

The courses of the Great Pyramid vary in thickness, as shown in this chart from
The Great Pyramid, by Peter Lemesurier, Element Books (1987):

Let's make an arbitrary assumption that the maximum stone volume to be raised in the Water Stairs is 1.5 cubic meters (1.5 x 2,611 Kg = 3,916 Kg or about 8,800 lbs). This means the float will have to displace 1.5 x 2,611/1,000 = 3.92 cubic meters of water (plus some for the weight of the float and sled). An equal amount of water will have to be displaced in the lockbox to lift the float creating a required volume of (3.92 x 2) or about 8 cubic meters (this is the volume of the float and displaced water).

Let's also take the example of Water Stair 1 as shown in Image 8.4. The Water Stair rests on courses 4 and 5 which have bases of 46 and 42 inches respectively, with heights of 39 and 38 inches respectively. This creates a cross sectional area of (77 x 88 sq. in) minus (39 x 42 sq. in) or 5,138 sq. inches. This is 5,138/144 = 35.68 SF or 35.68 x 0.0929 = 3.31 square meters. For this Water Stair to have a water volume of 8 cubic meters it would have to be 8/3.31 = 2.42 meters (8.06 feet) wide. The Water Stair support diagram (Image 8.3) shows a Water Stair 88 inches deep by 10 feet wide supported proportionally on the two lower courses.

Conclusion: The Float has to displace about 4 cubic meters, the lock box has a volume of about 8 cubic meters and the Water Stair unit will be approximately 8 feet deep by 10 feet wide.

A.16 – Bucket Brigade

We have already seen in Appendices A.2 and A.3 that the Sahara desertification was underway at the time of the building of the pyramids. Therefore it is likely that the pyramid builders had a 'Plan B' to raise water to the working level if the artesian well underperformed. Also from Appendix A.12 we know that the flow of water required was 22.76 cubic feet per minute over 20 years. Auxiliary human power could easily be used to raise water to the required level.

One cubic foot of water weighs about 62.4 lbs, easily carried by a human with a shoulder yoke and two goatskin bags balanced, one on each end, containing 31.2 lbs of water each. Twenty-two men working concurrently in shifts could provide this amount of water continuously.

If this is considered too heavy for full time labor we suggest that five gallons per man or 5 x 8.35 lbs = 41.75 lbs carried on a yoke with two 20.87 lb loads on each end would be easily accomplished. This would require about 33 men working continuously to deliver the required water flow and maybe a few more to make allowances for evaporation and leakage.

Conclusion: If lack of artesian water pressure made a 'Plan B' necessary to keep the working water level constant, it could easily be accomplished with a bucket brigade of between 22 and 33 men delivering their payload each minute.

A.17 – Volume of water in the Enclosure Pond

The Enclosure Pond has been estimated to be 10 meters wide at the base and enclosed the perimeter of the pyramid up to the height of the seventh stone course at 8.1 meters (319 inches). The width of the surface of the Pond at this height will be 10 meters plus 8.1/1.279* = 16.33 meters. The cross sectional area of the water is therefore (8.1 x 10) + (8.1 x 6.33)2 = 106.65 square meters. The total length of the pond is approximately 756 feet x 4 = 3,024 feet (921.95 meters) so the volume is 921.95 x 106.65 = 98,326 cubic meters.

*(Arc Tangent of 52 degrees [slope of side of pyramid]) = 1.279)

Conclusion: The full enclosure pond could contain an estimated 98,326 cubic meters of water which is enough water to fill the Mortuary Temple lock 7.68 times (see A.18).

141

A.18 – Volumes of water and stone in the lock system

Assuming the Mortuary Temple (lock) is 50 meters square (see Image 5.7) with 5 meter thick walls and 8 meters high the volume of stone in the walls is (50 x 5 x 2 x 8) + (40 x 5 x 2 x 8) = 7,200 cubic meters. The water capacity is 40 x 40 x 8 = 12,800 cubic meters.

Since there are no known cross-sectional dimensions of the "Causeway" we only have Herodotus' quote of 10 fathoms (60 feet [18 meters] wide) to use. We can combine this with the longitudinal sections of each lock shown in images 5.2 through 5.6 to estimate the volume of water (and stone) in the lock system. We will assume a cross section of the Causeway results in a ratio of water/stone of 2.5:1 (relative densities).

Lock #2 is approximately 193 meters long x 10 meters high x 18 meters wide divided by 2 (for the slope) = 17,370 cubic meters of which 12,407 is water and 4,963 is stone (see Image 5.4).

<u>Conclusion:</u> **Using data from the other images (5.2-5.6), lock volumes (of water and stone) are estimated to be as follows:**

Lock	Total Volume m³	Water Volume m³	Stone Volume m³
Mortuary Temple Lock #1	20,000	12,800	7,200
Lock #2	17,370	12,407	4,963
Lock #3	13,500	9,643	3,857
Lock #4	45,000	32,142	12,857
Lock #5	28,800	20,571	8,228
Lock #6	162,000	115,714	46,285
Valley Temple #7	20,000	12,800	7,200
TOTALS	306,670	216,077	90,590

A.19 – Volume of stone required for Phase 1 construction

The volume of stone in Phase 1 construction includes the volumes of the first seven courses, the Enclosure Wall, the "Mortuary Temple" Lock and the "Causeway" Lock construction down to and including the "Valley Temple" Lock.

If the first seven courses of the pyramid itself contain 16% of the approximately 2.6 million cubic meters of stone (see Appendix A.7) then the first seven courses contain 416,000 cubic meters.

Assuming the Enclosure Wall was 3 meters thick at the bottom and 1 meter thick at the top and 8 meters high this is a cross sectional area of 16 square meters. The length of the enclosure wall is 4 x 246 meters (226 + 20) or 984 meters. The volume of stone in the Enclosure Wall is estimated to be 984 x 16 or 15,744 cubic meters.

Lacking any meaningful evidence we will assume the content of stone in the Valley Temple is the same as the Mortuary Temple as shown in the above table.

Conclusion: The total amount of stone in the whole Phase 1 construction is estimated to be about 522,000 cubic meters.

A.20 – Delivery rate of stones for the Phase 1 Construction

According to Herodotus the Causeway and other site improvements took 10 years to build. This would mean a delivery rate (from above) of 522,000/10 or 52,200 cubic meters per year, or 143 cubic meters per day. Assuming a barge in the lock system is 10 meters long and about 5 meters wide carrying one layer of stones, it can deliver 50 cubic meters of stone per trip.

Conclusion: Delivering 150 cubic meters of stone per day could easily be accomplished using three barges 10 meters long and 5 meters wide; not huge barges.

A.21 – Delivery rate of stones for Phase 2 Construction

Phase 2 construction is all the stones above the seventh course. According to Herodotus the first 10 years were spent building the "Causeway" and the rest of the Phase 1 construction, so only 10 years was left to build the pyramid above the seventh course, which contained 84% of the 2.3 million stones. This equates to 1,932,000/10 = 193,200 stones placed each year, or 530 stones placed each day.

In our proposed Phase 2 delivery system there are four sets of Water Stairs, one up each of the pyramid edges with three being used to raise stones and the fourth to return sleds and waste down again. Each Water Stair has to lift 530/3 = 177 stones per day or one stone every 8 minutes.

Conclusion: Phase 2 construction would require each Water Stair to deliver 530/3 = 177 stones per day or about one stone every 8 minutes.

A.22 - The Dynamics of the Water Stairs

From A.15 we have a Water Stairs volume of 8 cubic meters. Using an 8 x 8 inch square wooden supply pipe it should be able to deliver about 2,000 gals per minute (see Table Appendix A.13) or 2000/7.481 = 271.62 cu ft per minute (1 gallon = 7.481 cu ft). The Water Stairs has a volume of about 8 cubic meters with half that volume taken up by the float, so about 4 cubic meters of water is needed to raise the stone and float. Four cubic meters of water is 4 x 35.31 cu ft = 141.24 cu ft so the 8 x 8 inch supply pipe will fill the Water Stairs in 141.24/271.62 = 0.52 minutes or 31.2 seconds.

The overall dynamics of the Water Stairs would have to include operator time to open and close valves, open and close gates and slide the stones on their sleds across to the next lockbox. We estimated a Water Stairs exchange rate of 3.5 minutes, which includes the 31.2 seconds fill time from above, (see Appendix A.28).

Since the Water Stairs only have to deliver about 84% (see Appendix A.7) of the stones in the pyramid there will only be 1,932,000 stones to deliver. Each of the three Water Stairs will have to lift only 644,000 stones to complete the pyramid. If it takes 3.5 minutes for each cycle, the time to deliver all stones is 644,000 x 3.5/60/24/365 = 4.28 years.

The Water Stairs were designed to accommodate the largest stone above the seventh course so it was built with a volume (weight) limit of, say, 1.5 cubic meters (2,611 Kg x 1.5 = 3,916 Kg or 8,800 lbs). From the prior estimates (Appendix A.7) courses 8 through 203 of the pyramid would be 84% of the volume of the total pyramid or 2.6 million cubic meters times 0.84 = 2,184,000 cubic meters. The three Water Stairs would each have to lift 72,184,000/3 = 28,000 cubic meters of stone. At 1.5 cubic meters of stone per cycle and 3.5 minutes per cycle, this would take 728,000/1.5 x 3.5/60/24/365 = 3.23 years operating 24 hours per day.

Using a 12 hour day this cycle time would double to 6.46 years. In the later stages of construction, especially above the 106th course where the stone size averages 22 inches, the Water Stairs could lift more than one stone at a time, thereby reducing the overall time even more.

Conclusion: The Water Stairs cycle time is estimated to be 3.5 minutes and operating around the clock the Water Stairs could lift all the stones above the pyramid's seventh course in about 3.23 years. If a 12-hour shift were used this time would expand to 6.46 years.

A.23 – Flow of the Nile River, Egypt

For illustrative purposes only, the River Nile has an average flow rate of 300 million cubic meters (m^3) per day or 208,300 m^3 per minute. From Appendix A.12 above, the volume of water required to balance the weight of the Great Pyramid is 6,524,642 m^3 say 6.5 million m^3. So the average flow of the Nile could lift 300/6.5 Great Pyramids per day, or 46.15 GPs per day or 1.92 GPs per hour!

A.24 – Flow of the Willamette River, Oregon

For illustrative purposes only, and a direct comparison to the River Nile, The Willamette River in Oregon has an average flow of 32,000 Cubic Feet/Second (CFS) or 1,920,000 CFM. In the maximum flood year of 1996 its flow was 460,000 CFS or 27,600,000 CFM. Using the average flow of the river the volume of water needed to balance the Great Pyramid is 230,385,104 cu ft (from previous calculations). At this rate the Willamette could lift 230,385,104 divided by 1,920,000 or one GP every 120 minutes or one every two hours! In the great flood of 1996 it could lift one GP every 8.35 minutes. Another interesting aspect of this comparison is that the two rivers are among the only large rivers in the world to flow from south to north.

A.25 - Notes on tunnels

In 1995, Zahi Hawass re-cleared the area in front of the Valley temple and in doing so, discovered that the causeways passed over tunnels that were framed with mudbrick walls and paved with limestone. These tunnels have a slightly convex profile resembling that of a boat. They formed a narrow corridor or canal running north-south. In front of the Sphinx Temple, the canal runs into a drain leading northeast, probably to a quay buried below the modern tourist plaza.

*The causeways connected the Nile canal with two separate entrances on the Valley temple facade that were sealed **by huge, single-leaf doors** probably made of cedar wood and hung on copper hinges. Each of these doorways was protected by a recumbent Sphinx. The northernmost of these portals was* dedicated to the goddess *Bastet*, while the southern portal was dedicated to *Hathor*.

Source: http://touregypt.net/featurestories/khafrep.htm

Tunnels under Giza Plateau. Aug. 13, 2009 *-- An enormous system of caves, chambers and tunnels lies hidden beneath the* Pyramids of Giza, *according to a British explorer who claims to have found the lost underworld of the pharaohs. Collins, who will detail his findings in the book "Beneath the Pyramids" to be published in September, tracked down the entrance to the mysterious underworld after reading the forgotten memoirs of a 19th century diplomat and explorer.*

Source: http://dsc.discovery.com/news/2009/08/13/caves-giza.html

A.26 - Notes on underground water causing problems

These natural reservoirs date back to thousands and even millions of years and they do not generally harm the antiquities. But man's modern manipulation of the underground water resources (such as the Aswan Dam agriculture, human waste sewage) had disturbed the natural Earth's system and thus results in these on surface concerns with the monuments. Water also trickles down from the surface of the ground which causes the rise in the level of water in these underground reservoirs. To eliminate this problem, the water level in the reservoirs has to be constantly measured especially at the places where monuments are located. Then the extent of the effect of water on the monuments has to be also measured and monitored. It is also important to study the old construction methods that Egyptians used to build their structures, for they were building these sites upon already ancient natural water reservoirs.

Source: http://www.touregypt.net/featurestories/newstoday06202001.htm

A.27 - Copper Pipes

"One of the more amazing historical uses for copper, illustrating its staying power, was the copper tubing in ancient Egypt. It appeared to be constructed like today's plumbing fixtures. Found in the tombs and temples of rulers, much of this tubing remains in an excellent, even functional, state more than 5000 years after its first use. This is because the very malleable copper is not as susceptible to corrosion as other metals, which is why it is still used today for pipes. Unlike plastic, copper does not give off fumes, melt, or burn. In

addition, copper has antibacterial properties that help to ward off microorganisms like those that cause Legionnaire's disease."

Source: - http://www.csa.com/discoveryguides/copper/overview.php

"When archeologists excavated the remains of a 4,500-year-old Egyptian funerary pyramid in 1994 they unearthed a sophisticated copper drainage system. Remarkably the copper pipes have survived to this day - an extraordinary example of copper's lifetime warranty."

Source: - http://www.copper.com.au/cdc/article.asp?CID=58&AID=264

Copper pipe was found inside the temple closest to the pyramid — which is called the "mortuary" Temple. Here priests assembled daily to present food and other objects as offerings to the dead King's spirit ... Experts speculate that the copper pipes, which extended some 330-yards along a causeway leading to another temple, were used to drain well water that was hand-carried into the temple to bathe the king's statues. These statues were anointed with oil as part of daily purification rituals.

Source:
http://www.copper.org/publications/newsletters/discover/dc_mar2005/pdf/dc_mar2005.pdf

A.28 – Estimate of Water Stairs Cycle Time

We estimated in Appendix A.22 that the time required to raise the float in the Lock Box with water from the Font Pond would be 31 seconds. Of course this is only part of the operation cycle so we will estimate a complete water stair operating cycle here.

Open valve	10 seconds
Raise float/stone	31
Shut valve	10
Open top gate	15
Move stone out	30
Close gates	15
Lower float	31
Open lower gate	15
Move stone in	30
	187
+15%	28

Conclusion: Water Stair Cycle time is 215 seconds, or about 3.5 minutes.

147

BIBLIOGRAPHY

Baines, John and Jaromir Malek. Atlas of Ancient Egypt. Equinox (Oxford) Ltd. 1980.

Bauval, Robert and Gilbert, Adrian. The Orion Mystery. New York. Three Rivers Press, 1994

Butzer, Karl W. Early Hydraulic Civilization in Egypt: A Study in Cultural Ecology. Chicago: University of Chicago Press, 1976.

Butzer, Karl W. Irrigation, Raised Fields and State Management: Wittfogel Redux? Antiquity, March 1996.

Clarke, Somers and R. Engelbach. Ancient Egyptian Construction and Architecture. Unabridged Dover (1990) republication of Ancient Egyptian Masonry: The Building Craft, originally published by Oxford University Press/Humphrey Milford, London, 1930.

Collins, Andrew. Beneath the Pyramids – Egypt's Greatest Secret Uncovered. Virginia Beach, Virginia: 4th Dimension Press, 2009

Deter, Arnold. Building in Egypt – Pharaonic Stone Masonry. New York Oxford: Oxford University Press, 1991

Ellis, Ralph. Thoth. Architect of the Universe, U.K. Edfu Books, 1997

Gilbert, Gregory P. Ancient Egyptian Sea Power and the Origin of Maritime Forces. Sea Power Centre — Australia, Department of Defense, Canberra ACT 2600. 2008

Heath, Robin and John Michell. The Lost Science of Measuring the Earth (Discovering the Sacred Geometry of the Ancients) Illinois: Adventures Unlimited Press, 2006.

Hornberger, George M. Elements of Physical Hydrology. Maryland: The Johns Hopkins University Press, 1998.

Hurst, H.E. The Hydrology of the Sobat and White Nile and the Topography of the Blue Nile and Atbara in the Nile Basin, Volume VIII. Cairo: Government Press, 1950.

Isler, Martin. Sticks, Stones and Shadows. University of Oklahoma Press. 2001

Jackson, Kevin and Stamp, Jonathan. Building the Great Pyramid Toronto: Firefly Books. 2003. Published to accompany the television program *Pyramid* on BBC1 2002.

Johnson, Peggy A. and P. Douglas Curtis. Water Balance of the Blue Nile River Basin in Ethiopia, Journal of Irrigation and Drainage Engineering, Vol. 120, No. 3 (May-June 1994).

Laboy, Samuel. A Civil Engineer Looks at the Great Pyramid, Alejo Ediciones, Lima, Peru, 2008.

Lehner, Mark. The Complete Pyramids (Solving the Ancient Mysteries), London: Thames and Hudson, Ltd. 1997.

Lehner, Mark and Wilma Wetterstrom. Giza Reports. The Giza Plateau Mapping Project, Massachusetts: Ancient Egypt Research Associates, 2007.

Lemesurier, Peter. Decoding the Great Pyramid London: Element Books, 1999.

Murray, G.W. Water from the Desert: Some Ancient Egyptian Achievements. Geographical Journal 121: 171-181, 1955.

Neubauer, W., M. Doneus, N. Studnicka, J Riegel. Combined High Resolution Laser Scanning and Photogrammetrical Documentation of the Pyramids at Giza. VIAS-Vienna Institute for Archaeological Science, Franz Klein-Gasse I/III, 1190 Vienna, Austria, Sep-Oct 2005.

Petrie, W. M. Flinders. The Pyramids and Temples of Gizeh. 1st ed. London: Field and Tuer; New York: Scribner & Welford, 1883. Republished online at *The Pyramids and Temples of Gizeh Online.* Ed. Ronald Birdsall, 2003. Rev. December 2, 2008. <http://www.ronaldbirdsall.com/gizeh>

Rawlinson, George. Herodotus, Histories. 1st Ed. 1858: Republished for Quality Paperback Book Club, 1997, Book-of-the-Month-Club, Inc., copyright 1997.

Said, Rushdi. The River Nile: Geology, Hydrology and Utilization. New York: Permagon Press, 1994.

Smyth, Charles Piazzi. Life and Work at the Great Pyramid. London: Wm. Isbister Ltd. 1880

Somers Clarke and R. Engelbach. Ancient Egyptian Construction and Architecture. Oxford University Press: Humphrey Milford, London, under the title *Ancient Egyptian Masonry: The Building Craft:* Republished by Dover Publications, Inc., 31 East 2nd Street, Mineola, N.Y. 11501.

Stocks, Denys A. Experiments in Egyptian Archaeology: Stoneworking Technology in Ancient Egypt. New York: Routledge, 2003.

Thurston, Harry. Secrets of the Sands. Doubleday Canada, a division of Random House of Canada Limited, 2003.

Tompkins, Peter. Secrets of the Great Pyramid. New York: Gallahad Books, 1997.

Warner, James W., Timothy K. Gates and Fatma A.R. Attia. Vertical Leakage in Egypt's Nile Valley; Estimation and Implications, in Journal of Irrigation and Drainage Engineering, Vol.117, pp 515-522 (July/August 1991).

AUTHORS' BIOGRAPHIES

Samuel R. Sampson, Architect

sam@oakfieldpublishers.com

Samuel was born in North Bend, Oregon, USA on August 25, 1946 and spent many youthful days building model cars, boats and airplanes and hunting and fishing the incomparable southern Oregon coast. He began formal education in Coos Bay, Oregon at Marshfield Senior High School, graduating in 1964.

As grandson of an itinerant Finnish carpenter and an enthusiastic model builder, Mr. Sampson went on to obtain a Bachelor of Architecture from the University of Oregon in 1970. In 1966-67, during his junior year in college, he studied abroad in Vienna, Austria concentrating on Architectural History, while touring many world-famous museums, landmarks and prominent architecture throughout Europe.

Mr. Sampson has practiced architecture professionally since 1974, and maintains licenses in both Oregon and Washington states. He has many years experience in designing and managing the architectural and engineering design teams for both governmental and private sector building projects of large magnitudes. In 2000, Samuel initiated a hobby by beginning his independent study of a long-standing architectural interest in Ancient Egypt and the Great Pyramid in particular.

Mr. Sampson's firm, Architectural Investigative Reports & Opinions (AIRO-LLC), provides traditional and specialty architectural services that include among others, constructability analyses and comprehensive evaluation and analysis of the condition of existing buildings, site work and infrastructure.

Michael N. Read, Engineer

mike@oakfieldpublishers.com

Michael was born in London, England on January 9, 1940 just after the outbreak of WWII and survived the London bombing Blitz by sleeping at night in an underground air raid shelter. In 1946 the family moved to Sandhurst, Berkshire and in 1951 he attended Woodley Hill Grammar School in Earley, near Reading, Berkshire.

In 1956 he graduated and went on to attend the Royal Aircraft Establishment Technical College (now Farnborough College of Technology). He graduated in 1961 and attended two more years part-time and was accepted as a Graduate of the Institution of Mechanical Engineers in 1963.

In the years 1961 to 1963 he worked at several aerospace companies in Bracknell, Berkshire and was involved with missile guidance systems. In 1966 he was recruited by The Boeing Company and moved to Seattle, Washington where he worked on avionics systems for the 747 airplane. He now is a General Certified Real Estate Appraiser licensed in Washington and Oregon and moved to Salem, Oregon in 2007 where he currently resides.

Here's hoping...

our book will be the start of a new dialogue about the Great Pyramid and Ancient Egypt that encourages your participation.

You're invited...

to experience the story in its entirety by "connecting the dots" of supporting evidence and to comment on any aspect of our book at:

www.floatingstonesbook.com

&

www.oakfieldpublishers.com

Thank you...

for purchasing and reading our book!

Made in the USA
Charleston, SC
26 October 2011